Introduction

Ladies and gentlemen of the jury, today, I present to you an idea that may seem radical at first glance. We're here to examine the concept that **God is Time itself**—that the very force guiding the unfolding of the universe, the structure of existence, and the rhythm of life is, in fact, an expression of the divine. We're here to consider the possibility that Time, Matter, and Space—forces we encounter every day—are not simply scientific phenomena but manifestations of God, Jesus, and the Holy Spirit.

Imagine the Bible not as a literal roadmap but as a collection of **parables and metaphors** designed to convey truths far beyond our everyday understanding. We'll look at familiar stories with fresh eyes, exploring the idea that God, as the creator, exists outside of creation, embodying Time—the force that shapes and orders all things. **Jesus, then, represents Matter,** the physical manifestation of the divine within our tangible world, and the **Holy Spirit as Space,** the connective presence that surrounds and fills everything.

Over the course of this book, I'll lay out evidence that supports this theory from a variety of angles: **biblical interpretations, scientific principles, spiritual insights, and human experience.** We'll look at scriptures not simply for their literal meaning, but for the hidden truths that have perhaps been overlooked or misunderstood over the centuries. We'll also dive into scientific discoveries about time, space, and matter, finding ways these insights might align with, rather than contradict, our understanding of God.

I'll ask you to suspend disbelief, to allow curiosity and open-mindedness to guide you through this exploration. As we examine these ideas, I'll challenge assumptions about God, faith, and existence itself. By the end of this journey, my hope is that you will see a divine framework that brings together **faith and science** in a way that adds depth to both, offering a new way to experience the sacred.

So, with this foundation laid, let's begin to examine the evidence. Together, we'll explore what it truly means if **God is Time, Jesus is Matter, and the Holy Spirit is Space.** I ask you only to keep an open mind and see where this journey takes us.

Prologue

What if the reason you don't believe is because everything you've been told was wrong? Not necessarily out of malice or intention, but perhaps from centuries of misunderstanding. Interpretations of the divine have been passed down, adapted, and reshaped, spawning countless religions that share a common origin yet diverge in their view of God. Imagine, for a moment, that these interpretations missed something essential, and that the God you seek isn't a distant figure with a white beard on a throne in the sky.

Maybe you've never questioned it, or perhaps you've dismissed the idea of God altogether. But what if your disbelief has more to do with the way God has been framed than with God's true nature? What if God isn't just a supreme being above us but something far closer, something more woven into the essence of life itself?

In this book, we'll challenge familiar images and explore a fresh perspective, one rooted in both **faith** and **science**. We'll consider the idea that **God could be Time itself**—the force that moves all things forward, that shapes our experiences and gives life its structure. What if **Jesus represents Matter**, the tangible form of divinity, and the **Holy Spirit is Space**, the presence that connects and surrounds us? These ideas may seem unconventional, even radical, but they offer a new way to understand the universe and our place in it.

This journey isn't about dismantling beliefs or constructing a new doctrine. It's an invitation to think differently, to view the divine as something profoundly intertwined with existence. Each chapter will explore these themes through the lenses of science, spirituality, and physical reality, piecing together a vision of God that transcends traditional interpretations.

Maybe everything you've been told wasn't quite right. But the one thing that might be true? That all dogs really do go to heaven. Let's begin this exploration together, embracing curiosity and challenging old perceptions. Whether you're here from a place of faith or skepticism, you're invited to walk this path and discover what it means if God is not simply a distant force, but the very flow of time that shapes all things.

Chapter 1: The Beginning of Time, Matter, and Space

"Time is but the stream I go a-fishing in." – Henry David Thoreau

Introduction: The Beginning of Everything

In the beginning, there was nothing. No stars, no planets, no time ticking by. And then, with a single act, everything came into being—time, matter, and space. The Bible and science both try to describe this event in their own ways. The Bible tells us that God spoke, and creation began. Science speaks of the Big Bang, an explosion that set the universe into motion. But perhaps these two accounts aren't as different as they seem.

Both stories agree on this: there was nothing, and then, something happened, and the universe was created. That 'something'—whether it was God's voice or an explosion of energy—marked the beginning of time itself.

God as Time: Elohim and Yahweh

To truly understand this moment of creation, we need to look deeper into the nature of God. In the Bible, God is often referred to by different names, each revealing something about His nature. The name **Elohim**, which appears in the very first verse of the Bible, is a plural form that hints at complexity. It could be seen as a reference to the Trinity—the Father, Son, and Holy Spirit—or it could represent the three fundamental elements of creation: time, matter, and space.

Elohim could symbolize how these elements work together to form the universe, with God as the most high, governing over them. **Yahweh**, on the other hand, is a more personal name for God. It is linked to the idea of 'I AM,' or the one who is, reflecting God's eternal and unchanging nature. In this theory, **Yahweh represents God as Time**, the eternal force that governs matter and space, always present, always in control.

Adam and Eve: The Building Blocks of Humanity

Let's delve deeper into the creation of Adam and Eve, not just as biblical figures but as symbols that align with the foundational elements of life. The name **Adam** (אָדָם) in Hebrew is connected to **'adamah'** (הָאֲדָמָה), meaning 'ground' or 'earth,' emphasizing his origin from the earth—or matter. If we extend this metaphor, Adam represents the 'atom,' the basic building block of matter and, by extension, humanity.

Eve (הַוָּה, Chavvah or Chava), whose name comes from the Hebrew word **'chayah'** (הָיָה), meaning 'to live' or 'to give life,' symbolizes the dynamic and life-giving force that complements matter. This aligns with the Genesis narrative in which Eve is described as "the mother of all living" (Genesis 3:20). The Greek translation of her name in the Septuagint became **Eva**, and this evolved into **Eve** in English.

But there's more to Eve's story that resonates with scientific discovery. The concept of **Mitochondrial Eve** refers to the most recent common matrilineal ancestor of all living humans. This "Eve" is traced through **mitochondrial DNA (mtDNA)**, passed down from mother to child. Scientific research indicates that this ancestral woman lived in Africa, aligning with the understanding that humanity originated from that continent. While this Mitochondrial Eve isn't directly related to the biblical Eve, the shared concept of a common maternal lineage echoes the idea of Eve as the "mother of all living."

In this metaphorical framework, if **Adam** represents the fundamental unit of matter, then **Eve** could represent **DNA**, the carrier of genetic information that gives rise to life. DNA embodies the potential for reproduction, diversity, and the blueprint for humanity. This notion enriches the symbolic interpretation of Eve as more than just a counterpart to Adam; she is essential for the perpetuation and complexity of life. Just as Adam symbolizes the raw material—the atom—Eve represents the life force and information that animates and propagates matter.

The Big Bang and Creation: Two Perspectives

From a scientific perspective, the universe began with the **Big Bang**, about 13.8 billion years ago. In that moment, time, matter, and space came into existence. Before that, there was no time, no matter, no space—only a point of infinite density and temperature. When this point expanded, it gave birth to the universe as we know it.

In the Bible's account of creation, God spoke, and the universe was formed. The act of speaking, in a way, can represent the Big Bang. Both stories tell us that nothing existed—and then, in a single moment, everything changed. God's voice can be seen as the spark that set time into motion, just as the Big Bang was the spark that began the universe's expansion.

Time, Matter, and Space: The Foundations of Creation

With time in motion, the next two elements had to follow—matter and space. Matter is the physical substance of the universe, and space is the canvas where matter exists. The Bible says, "In the beginning, God created the heavens and the earth." The heavens represent space, while the earth represents matter. Time was already in place, and now matter and space were joining the stage.

This mirrors modern science, where time, matter, and space were all born from the same event. Time governs how matter behaves within the framework of space.

The Creation of Adam: Matter Takes Form

The Bible tells us that Adam was created from dust or dirt, and that Eve was formed from Adam's rib. This ancient story can be seen as a way of explaining that Adam was created from matter—from the physical substance of the earth. God breathed life into Adam, bringing time and matter together to create life.

Adam's creation from dirt symbolizes matter in its raw form, while God's breath represents the entry of time into matter, setting it into motion. Eve's creation from Adam's rib reflects the idea that matter can be transformed, just as we see in the rest of creation—matter is always changing, always taking on new forms, but it remains matter. This transformation mirrors the formation of molecules from atoms, suggesting Eve's role as the life-giving force derived from the basic building block.

Relativity and the Nature of Time

Einstein's Theory of Relativity tells us that time is not fixed. It can stretch or contract depending on the conditions of gravity and speed. This flexibility of time aligns with the idea that **God as Time** governs the universe in ways that are beyond our human understanding. God isn't bound by the linear progression of time as we are. He moves through time, shaping creation without being constrained by it.

For us, time moves forward, from past to present to future. But for God, time is like a book—He sees the whole story at once. This is why God's timing often feels different from our own. We experience time as a sequence, while God sees all moments at once.

Reflection and Meditative Questions

- **Reflection**: How does the idea of God as Time influence your view of creation and your own life? Does it change how you think about the beginning of everything, and how events unfold in your daily life?

- **Meditation**: Take a moment to reflect on the relationship between time and creation. How might your perception of God change if you understood time as the canvas for His actions? What does it mean for you to trust in God's timing?

- **Practical Application**: This week, focus on an area of your life where you feel uncertain about timing. Consider how trusting in God's timing could bring you peace and try to reflect on moments when things happened at just the right time.

Chapter 2: Time as God (The Father)

"Time is an illusion." – Albert Einstein

The Concept of Time Beyond Perception

Time is something we often take for granted, yet it governs every moment of our existence. It's the unseen force that drives the cycle of life, from the rising of the sun to the changing of the seasons, and from birth to death. We measure time in hours, days, and years, but what if time itself is more than just a construct to track our existence? What if time is, in fact, the very essence of God, a divine force that transcends our understanding?

The Bible frequently describes God as eternal, existing from "everlasting to everlasting" (Psalm 90:2). This timeless nature of God suggests that He is not bound by the linear flow of past, present, and future. Instead, God encompasses all of time simultaneously. This idea aligns with Einstein's theory of relativity, which suggests that time is not an absolute constant but is flexible and influenced by factors such as gravity and speed. In a spiritual sense, this perspective helps us understand how God could see and influence all moments at once, weaving together the story of existence seamlessly.

Time as the Foundation of Creation

If we consider God as Time, then His act of creation becomes even more profound. The book of Genesis begins with, "In the beginning, God created the heavens and the earth" (Genesis 1:1). This declaration marks not just the start of creation, but the initiation of time itself. Time sets the stage for everything else to unfold—matter and space could not exist without it.

From a scientific standpoint, time plays an essential role in the birth and expansion of the universe. According to modern cosmology, time, matter, and space were all intertwined from the moment of the Big Bang. Without time, there would be no forward movement of events, no unfolding of life or creation. When viewed through this lens, God's spoken word in Genesis symbolizes the spark that set time into motion, echoing the scientific concept of the Big Bang as the initial moment when time began.

The Importance of Divine Timing

The concept of divine timing is woven throughout scripture and has profound implications for our understanding of life and spirituality. Ecclesiastes 3:1 states, "To everything there is a season, a time for every purpose under heaven." This passage underscores that every event unfolds according to a higher plan, governed by God as Time. In the realm of physics, we understand that time's flow can appear to vary, stretching and contracting depending on external conditions like gravity. This is exemplified by the phenomenon of time dilation, where time moves more slowly near a massive object or at higher speeds. Just as time can shift in the physical realm, divine timing may feel different to us but is always in accordance with a greater plan.

In astrology, the concept of timing is also significant. Planetary movements and alignments are believed to influence human affairs and are used to interpret the best moments for action, reflection, or change. While astrology doesn't directly connect to the idea of God as Time, it mirrors the belief that timing holds deep spiritual meaning and impacts our journey. Just as the planets move in their courses with precision, life events unfold in their appointed time, suggesting a universal rhythm that God oversees.

God's Relationship with Time: The Divine Clockmaker

The metaphor of God as a clockmaker, often used to describe how He set the universe in motion and continues to guide it, becomes even more profound when we consider Him as Time itself. Time is the governing force that provides structure, rhythm, and continuity to existence. Without time, there would be no change, no growth, and no progression. As Time, God is not only the creator but the sustainer of the universe, moving it forward and ensuring that everything happens at its appointed time.

Divine timing becomes particularly relevant when we consider how life events unfold. We often hear phrases like, "Trust in God's timing," especially during moments of waiting or uncertainty. This isn't just a comforting saying; it is a reminder that time itself holds divine wisdom. In a world where we are constantly chasing schedules and deadlines, viewing time as a sacred and orchestrated force can change how we approach our lives. Recognizing God as Time implies that every second carries divine significance, each heartbeat a moment charged with purpose.

Free Will and Divine Timing

One question that often arises when discussing God and time is the relationship between free will and divine intervention. If God is Time, does that mean our actions are predetermined? The answer lies in the unique nature of time itself. While time is a constant force, it allows for infinite possibilities. We make choices within the flow of time, and those choices affect our personal timelines and potentially the timelines of others. Yet, God, as Time, can see all possible outcomes, guiding us while still allowing us the freedom to choose.

Think about it this way: time provides the stage on which we act. We can make choices that lead us down different paths, but time (God) remains the framework that supports these choices. The intricate web of decisions and consequences exists within the divine structure of time. This is why many people of faith say, "Everything happens in God's time." It's not that our lives are controlled by a puppeteer, but that the divine nature of time ensures that everything unfolds as it should, even when we cannot see the full picture.

The Physics of Divine Timing: A Deeper Dive

Understanding the physics behind time adds another layer to this concept. According to Einstein's general theory of relativity, massive objects like planets and stars bend spacetime, creating gravitational fields that affect how time flows. This means that time is not uniform throughout the universe. Just as time slows down near a black hole due to immense gravity, divine timing can feel slow or accelerated in our lives, depending on our perspective.

Quantum physics also offers an intriguing view of time. In the quantum realm, particles can exist in states of superposition, meaning they hold multiple potentials until observed. This mirrors the concept that God, as Time, holds all potential outcomes until they are realized. It suggests that reality itself is a tapestry of possibilities that unfold in divine timing.

The Spiritual Implications of Divine Timing

Understanding God as Time changes how we view patience, waiting, and the unfolding of our lives. It suggests that delays, setbacks, and unexpected changes are not merely random occurrences but part of a divine schedule. When we say, "Everything happens for a reason," we are acknowledging the sacredness of time and trusting that each moment has its purpose.

For example, have you ever experienced moments where an unexpected delay kept you from a negative outcome or a sudden opportunity arose at just the right time? These instances, often attributed to luck or coincidence, can be seen as evidence of divine timing. This understanding can provide comfort and perspective, especially in moments of struggle or waiting. Trusting in God as Time means embracing the belief that events unfold in perfect synchrony, even when they don't match our personal timelines. The idea that God is Time encourages us to let go of our need for control and to trust in the unfolding of life as it's meant to be.

Time and Astrology: A Universal Dance

In astrology, the movement of celestial bodies reflects the passing of time and its influence on human experiences. The cycles of planets, particularly Saturn (often called the "Lord of Time"), signify phases of growth, lessons, and endings. While astrology is not a religious practice, its deep connection with the timing of events provides an interesting parallel to the concept of divine timing. The universe, with its precise dance of planets and stars, can be seen as a testament to the order and intention that God, as Time, imbues into creation.

Astrology's emphasis on timing—whether through retrogrades, eclipses, or planetary returns—can serve as a reminder of how life is influenced by the unseen forces of time and space. Just as ancient civilizations used the stars to guide their actions and understand their place in the cosmos, acknowledging God as Time allows us to see each moment as part of a greater, divinely orchestrated plan.

Reflection and Meditative Questions

- **Reflection**: How does thinking of God as Time influence your understanding of divine timing and the unfolding of your own life's journey? Can you think of moments when divine timing played a role in significant life events?

- **Meditation**: Consider moments in your life where timing played a crucial role. How might those moments reflect the idea that God, as Time, was guiding events to align perfectly with His plan?

- **Practical Application**: Practice mindfulness by viewing each moment as an encounter with the divine. This week, reflect on how you spend your time and whether it aligns with your spiritual beliefs and long-term goals.

Chapter 3: Jesus as Matter – The Tangible Presence of the Divine

"Everything flows, nothing stays still." – Heraclitus

Imagine holding a stone in your hand, feeling its solid weight, its unchanging form. Now, imagine that same stone after years under a flowing river—it may erode, transform, but it never disappears entirely. This is the nature of **matter**—constantly in flux, yet ever-present in some form. Matter is not static; it's dynamic, always moving, changing, shifting, but ultimately enduring. And in the Trinity, **Jesus represents this very essence of matter**.

Matter forms the foundation of the universe—every particle, every living thing, and even us. In the person of Jesus, God made Himself matter, giving the divine a tangible form that we could see, touch, and understand. The incarnation is a revelation: **God doesn't just create matter; He inhabits it**.

The Eternal Transformation of Matter

One of the foundational principles in physics is the **law of conservation of matter**. It states that matter can neither be created nor destroyed; it only changes forms. This principle is mirrored in Jesus' life, death, and resurrection. Jesus wasn't simply destroyed on the cross—He was transformed, revealing a new form beyond the physical limits of matter as we understand it.

Jesus' transformation serves as a reminder that **matter has an eternal quality**, constantly changing but never disappearing. In the same way that water cycles from liquid to vapor to ice, **Jesus' resurrection shows matter transcending death**, offering a new perspective on transformation as a divine promise.

Physics and Matter's Unseen Potential

In quantum mechanics, particles of matter have mysterious qualities that defy logic. **Quantum particles** can exist in multiple places at once, and they can shift states in an instant. These particles operate beyond the everyday laws of matter we're familiar with—suggesting that the physical world is far more **complex and interconnected** than we can see.

Through Jesus, God reveals that matter has a **divine potential** that we're only beginning to understand. When He walked on water or turned water into wine, Jesus showed that **matter could be transformed by the divine presence**. Just as particles can behave in unexpected ways, **Jesus' miracles** demonstrate that the material world is full of possibilities beyond our comprehension. His actions invite us to see matter as sacred, as part of a greater spiritual tapestry.

The Interconnectedness of Matter in Astrology and the Cosmos

Astrology, though often seen as symbolic, speaks to an interconnectedness between the material bodies of the cosmos—planets, stars, and moons—and the events on earth. Ancient beliefs held that celestial matter, far away though it may be, has an influence on earthly life. In the same way, Jesus, as the Son, represents a connection between God and creation, bringing divine presence into the physical world.

Our physical reality is intertwined with cosmic matter; **stars give birth to elements**, which in turn form planets and, ultimately, life itself. Jesus as Matter reflects this **interconnected nature**. Through Him, God entered into creation and aligned divine purpose with the physical laws of the universe.

Biblical Miracles: Mastery Over Matter

The Bible presents Jesus as not only a teacher but also as someone who could control and transform matter itself. Each miracle reflects a **revelation of divine mastery over the physical**:

- **Turning water into wine** shows a transformation of matter, suggesting that physical elements can become new, even elevated forms.

- **Walking on water** defies physical boundaries, revealing that Jesus was not bound by the material limits that govern our daily experiences.

- **Feeding the multitude** with a few loaves and fishes demonstrates a miraculous multiplication, a reflection of abundance within divine matter.

These miracles aren't simply supernatural events; they serve as **parables in matter**, teaching us that the physical world, too, is capable of divine transformation.

Jesus as the Bridge Between Spirit and Matter

In the Greek key, we see an unbroken line, a **symbol of eternity and continuity**. Jesus as Matter embodies this continuous connection between God and creation, an unbreakable bridge. Matter is sacred because God entered it, transforming our understanding of the physical world as a vessel for the divine.

Jesus reminds us that **matter is not simply "stuff"**; it's a manifestation of God's presence. Through His life, we're shown that physical existence itself holds meaning, and that our experiences, challenges, and transformations are all part of this divine continuum.

Reflective Prompts

- **How does understanding Jesus as Matter change your view of the physical world?** Reflect on ways the material world is intertwined with divine creativity and presence.

- **Consider the miracles of Jesus in terms of transformation.** How do these miracles illustrate the divine potential of matter? Think of them as metaphors for transformation in your own life.

- **Think about the interconnectedness of matter and spirit.** How might this concept change how you view your own body, surroundings, and daily experiences?

Chapter 4: The Holy Spirit as Space – The Divine Presence That Connects All

"Space and time are the framework within which the mind is constrained to construct its experience of reality." – Immanuel Kant

Imagine entering a vast, open field. Though it seems empty, it's alive with potential, holding endless possibilities within it. This is how we can view **space**, not as emptiness, but as a presence that allows things to exist, move, and interact. In the Trinity, the **Holy Spirit** can be seen as this essential space—a divine presence that fills all things, connecting them in one continuous, life-giving medium.

Kant's reflection reminds us that space and time are more than physical dimensions; they're the fabric of experience itself. **What if the Holy Spirit is like space, creating the framework in which God and creation meet?** Much like space enables matter to move and time to progress, the Holy Spirit enables divine connection and interaction.

The Nature of Space: An Essential Presence

In our universe, space is everywhere. It's the vast expanse that holds galaxies, stars, planets, and all physical reality. Without space, there would be no room for matter to exist or time to unfold. The Holy Spirit operates in a similar way, **creating a sacred space where God's presence flows freely** through all creation.

Space isn't passive; it's dynamic. It bends, expands, and shapes itself around the objects within it, much like the **Holy Spirit fills, moves, and unites** everything it touches. The Spirit as Space is a reminder that God's presence isn't confined to a single location; it permeates every inch of existence, touching every part of life, holding everything together.

Astrological Insights: The Space that Binds

In astrology, planets move through space, each holding symbolic influence. Celestial bodies are separated by vast distances, yet they exist in relation to one another, creating patterns and influences. This cosmic dance can be seen as an analogy for the **Holy Spirit's role as the binding space** that enables unity. Just as stars and planets influence each other across space, the Holy Spirit connects us all, allowing relationships, events, and energies to flow together in a cosmic framework.

Space isn't just a void; it's a **bridge between objects**. Through the Holy Spirit, God's essence flows across the "space" between souls, linking us with divine influence and connection.

Physics of Space: The Expanding Universe and the Holy Spirit's Reach

The scientific discovery that **space is constantly expanding** mirrors the expansive reach of the Holy Spirit. Space is not fixed; it's always stretching, allowing for growth and the creation of new stars, planets, and galaxies. Similarly, the Holy Spirit is described in the Bible as moving over the waters of creation, constantly **bringing life, renewal, and transformation**.

In **cosmology**, space-time is a fabric that warps around matter, shaping how things move and interact. If we view the Holy Spirit as this space, it suggests that **God's Spirit is actively shaping our reality**, guiding us toward divine purpose and meaning. Just as space holds the universe in a delicate balance, the Holy Spirit holds us in connection, allowing God's presence to flow into every moment and place.

Biblical Metaphors: Wind, Breath, and the Spirit That Fills All

In the Bible, the Holy Spirit is often described as **wind** or **breath**—an invisible force that brings life and energy. Just as wind moves through open spaces, **the Spirit moves through creation**, unseen but deeply felt. In Genesis, the Spirit hovers over the waters, filling the primordial space with the potential for life.

When Jesus spoke of the Holy Spirit, He described it as a helper and comforter, an unseen presence that would guide and fill the disciples. The Holy Spirit is both **constant and dynamic**, like the space that surrounds us. It's a living, breathing presence, creating room for God's influence and love to dwell among us.

The Greek Key and the Holy Spirit's Unbroken Continuity

Returning to the **Greek key**, its continuous line reminds us of the **Holy Spirit's eternal presence**. Just as the key's design weaves in an unbroken path, the Holy Spirit is an unending connection that binds all creation. This motif of continuity suggests that the Spirit's influence isn't temporary; it's woven into the fabric of existence, moving in cycles that bring renewal and unity.

The Holy Spirit as Space invites us to see all of creation as a **sacred continuum**, where every person, place, and thing is interconnected by divine presence. Space is not empty; it is filled with the Spirit's presence, allowing us to encounter God in every moment and every place.

Reflective Prompts

- **Consider the Holy Spirit as the space within which all things connect.** How does this perspective change your understanding of divine presence?

- **Reflect on moments where you felt surrounded by peace or comfort.** Could these experiences be an encounter with the Holy Spirit as the connective "space" around you?

- **Think about the expansion of the universe and the Holy Spirit's reach.** How might this reflect God's endless capacity to hold, nurture, and guide creation?

Chapter 5: The Trinity and the Universe – A Divine Blueprint

"Time present and time past are both perhaps present in time future, and time future contained in time past." – T.S. Eliot

Picture this: you're at a cosmic dinner party, seated with three guests—Time, Matter, and Space. Time is wearing a wise old cloak, nodding slowly as it measures every word. Matter is busy rearranging the furniture, shaping everything in sight, while Space lounges comfortably, stretching out and making room for everyone to breathe. This trio doesn't just work together—they're inseparable, constantly interacting and playing off each other. This is the **Trinity**: a divine dance of **Time, Matter, and Space**, mirroring the Father, the Son, and the Holy Spirit.

In the same way that the universe can't exist without these three elements, the Holy Trinity represents the **essential structure** of both physical and spiritual reality. **God the Father** as Time governs the flow of events. **Jesus the Son** as Matter gives form to God's will. And the **Holy Spirit as Space** fills every moment with divine presence. Together, they form a **cosmic blueprint** for everything that exists.

The Trinity as the Framework of Existence

In physics, **spacetime** is a unified concept that blends space and time into a single fabric, with matter shaping its curves and bends. The Trinity functions similarly— each member plays a vital role, but none can be separated from the whole. This cosmic trinity creates a framework that holds the universe together, a web of **interconnected forces** that reflect God's unified nature.

Imagine trying to separate time from space or space from matter—it's impossible. Just like the Holy Trinity, these elements can only function as a whole. This divine blueprint reveals a profound truth: God's presence isn't divided. It's unified, a seamless blend of roles that shape reality itself. This is the **Trinity in action**, working continuously behind the scenes.

How the Universe Mirrors the Trinity

In the natural world, we see reflections of this divine structure everywhere. Consider the **three states of matter**: solid, liquid, and gas. Just as water can transform from ice to liquid to vapor, God's presence can be experienced in different forms—Father, Son, and Holy Spirit—yet remains fundamentally the same. The Trinity is present in the **three dimensions** of space, the **three stages of life** (birth, growth, death), and the **three acts of a story** (beginning, middle, end).

Even the **Big Bang**, the scientific explanation for the universe's creation, has a trinity-like quality. The explosion of energy created **time, space, and matter** in an instant, mirroring the simultaneous roles of the Trinity. The Father (Time) initiated the event, the Son (Matter) took form, and the Spirit (Space) expanded to hold everything together. This divine pattern is built into the very structure of the cosmos.

The Spiritual Implications of the Trinity

If the Trinity forms the foundation of the universe, what does that mean for us? It means we're living in a world that's **divinely structured**—a place where time, matter, and space work in harmony, just as the Father, Son, and Holy Spirit do. **Time guides us**, **matter grounds us**, and **space gives us room to grow**. Every moment, every breath, every experience is a chance to encounter the divine.

The Trinity isn't just an abstract concept; it's a living reality that shapes how we move, think, and feel. It's why time brings healing, why matter can transform, and why space allows connection. By understanding the universe as a reflection of the Trinity, we can see life itself as a spiritual journey—a path guided by divine order, unfolding perfectly in every moment.

Finding Humor in the Divine Structure

You might be thinking, "Okay, so the universe is a divine trinity. But what does that mean for my daily life?" Picture this: every time you're stuck in traffic, it's not just an annoyance—it's an opportunity to appreciate **God as Time**, moving you along at a divine pace. Every time you spill coffee on yourself, it's a reminder that **Matter** is unpredictable, but also transformable (just like your mood after a good cup). And every time you can't find your keys, well, that's **Space** playing hide-and-seek. The divine has a sense of humor, too.

The beauty of the Trinity is that it's not just about cosmic mysteries—it's about the small, everyday moments that reveal **God's presence**. Time, matter, and space aren't just philosophical ideas; they're the framework of our daily lives, shaping every experience, whether it's profound or mundane.

Reflective Prompts

- **Consider how the Trinity reflects your own life.** Where do you see Time, Matter, and Space working together in your day-to-day activities?

- **Reflect on moments when you felt connected to something greater.** Could this be an encounter with the divine structure of the universe?

- **Think about how the Trinity shapes your understanding of God.** How does this perspective change your view of spirituality and reality?

Chapter 6: Time's Role in Redemption – The Journey Through Divine Timing

"Time is the number of movement in respect of before and after." – Aristotle

Imagine life as a massive, intricate clock, ticking along with each person, each decision, moving its hands forward. Each moment brings something new—growth, change, healing. And through it all, **time plays a key role** in our journey toward redemption. The concept of God as Time suggests that every second holds divine purpose, nudging us closer to transformation.

In Christian theology, redemption is a journey, a slow process that unfolds in time. **God's timing** is integral to this process, as He patiently waits for the right moment, the perfect unfolding of events. Time doesn't merely pass; it carries us along, shaping us through experiences that draw us closer to divine purpose. In this sense, time itself becomes a medium through which God's plan of redemption takes shape.

Time as a Healer: A Biblical Perspective

Throughout the Bible, **time is portrayed as an essential element of redemption**. Jesus' life, death, and resurrection are all part of a carefully timed plan. In **Galatians 4:4**, we read, "When the fullness of time had come, God sent forth His Son." This phrase, "fullness of time," speaks to the idea that divine timing isn't rushed—it's perfectly orchestrated, with each event playing a role in a greater plan.

Consider the Israelites wandering in the desert for forty years. While it might seem excessive, this period served as a time of purification, a chance to forge a closer relationship with God. The journey to redemption often takes time because it's a process of learning, growing, and refining. In waiting, in moving through time, we are given the opportunity to experience God's transformative power.

The Ripple Effect of Decisions and Divine Timing

Every choice we make has a ripple effect, stretching out and impacting the lives of others, often in ways we can't even see. Imagine making a single decision, like **choosing to drive after drinking**. This one choice could affect not only your life but also the lives of others on the road, changing their timelines, their futures, and even the lives of people they interact with down the line. A single moment can alter countless futures, creating ripples that continue indefinitely.

This is where God as Time, Matter, and Space—the Trinity—can work to guide, protect, and ultimately help redeem us. Time, as God, moves us forward, but our choices shape the direction. Matter, as Jesus, shows us the importance of our actions in the material world, emphasizing that what we do with our bodies and choices matters deeply. Space, as the Holy Spirit, surrounds us, creating moments of intervention and grace that sometimes shield us from the impact of our decisions.

Divine Interventions: The Holy Trinity in Action

Consider the example of a traffic light turning red just as you approach it. While frustrating at the moment, that brief delay might be keeping you from harm's way—perhaps even from crossing paths with a drunk driver. This unseen protection isn't random; it's the Holy Trinity at work. The **Holy Spirit as Space** creates that moment of separation, shielding you in a way you may never realize.

In this way, **the Holy Trinity comes together to protect and guide us**. Time, through divine timing, ensures that certain events align or diverge. Matter, through Jesus, gives significance to the physical choices we make. Space, through the Holy Spirit, creates a divine buffer, allowing or preventing interactions that shape our lives.

Sometimes, we may never know how many dangers we've been spared because of these divine interventions. Other times, we're left wondering why we weren't stopped, why certain tragedies happen despite our hopes. But if God is Time, then even in our painful moments, there's a promise that these events are leading toward a greater purpose—a path where redemption and healing are ultimately possible.

The Physics of Time and Healing

From a scientific perspective, **time is essential to the healing process**. The body needs time to recover from injury, and emotional wounds often take even longer to mend. Time has a way of gently softening our pain, giving us the space to heal and grow stronger. This is true not only in the physical world but also in the spiritual realm. **Time, as God, becomes a healer**, giving us room to forgive, to reconcile, and to transform.

Just as a broken bone needs weeks to repair, the soul often needs time to heal from loss, anger, or betrayal. The process may feel slow, but each moment carries us closer to wholeness. God, as Time, walks with us through these seasons of change, reminding us that redemption isn't instant but a gradual unfolding of grace.

Time, Redemption, and Divine Patience

If we consider God as Time, then every moment is an invitation to grow and change. **Redemption is a journey, not a destination**—it's a path that requires patience, reflection, and openness. Just as time allows for the gradual blossoming of flowers or the slow growth of trees, God's redemptive work in our lives unfolds one moment at a time.

Sometimes we question why certain things take so long. "Why doesn't God act sooner?" But if **God is Time**, then divine patience is part of the process. In the waiting, we find lessons, we gain perspective, and we come to understand that **God's timing is perfect**. The redemption of a soul, like the formation of a mountain, is a gradual, purposeful act that cannot be rushed.

Time as the Builder of the New Earth

The Bible speaks of a **new earth** that will one day replace the current world. This vision isn't about an instant change but a slow, ongoing transformation. As we move through time, each act of kindness, forgiveness, and compassion contributes to the building of this new reality. If God is Time, then God is also the architect of this future world, working patiently, guiding humanity toward redemption.

In this vision of a new earth, only those who choose goodness and compassion will remain. The process of redemption is, in a sense, a refining fire that slowly separates the good from the bad. Time will eventually bring about a world where evil no longer exists—a new earth filled only with souls who have embraced divine love and light.

Humor in the Waiting: God's Timetable vs. Ours

We often find ourselves in moments where we're impatient, frustrated by how long things take. We joke about God's timing, but there's a humorous irony in it—our "right now" is rarely the same as God's. Imagine calling divine customer service, only to be put on eternal hold! God's timetable, if God is Time, doesn't follow our agendas, but that's part of the beauty and mystery of faith.

As humans, we tend to want everything immediately. We crave instant gratification, but God, as Time, invites us to a slower rhythm. Perhaps God, in divine wisdom, wants us to learn that not everything needs to happen in an instant. Redemption, growth, and healing—all of these take time, and that's okay. Sometimes, the wait itself is a blessing.

Reflective Prompts

- **Consider a moment when an unexpected delay or change seemed to protect or guide you.** How might this have been an example of divine timing at work?

- **Reflect on the ripple effect of your choices.** How does seeing your decisions as part of a larger timeline of redemption change your perspective on your actions?

- **Think of a long-term goal or dream.** How does viewing time as part of God's plan help you approach it with patience and faith?

Chapter 7: Time and Prophecy – The Divine Blueprint of What's to Come

"The past, like the future, is indefinite and exists only as a spectrum of possibilities." – Stephen Hawking

Imagine standing at the edge of a vast timeline, looking both forward and backward. The future is a canvas, partially hidden, stretching out before us as a collection of potential paths and outcomes. This idea of **time and prophecy** invites us to consider a divine perspective—one where **God as Time** sees every possibility, every path, and every potential choice.

Prophecy in the Bible isn't just about foretelling events; it's about showing that God, in His role as Time, holds every outcome in His hands. Prophets didn't simply predict; they were tuned into a divine vision that allowed them glimpses into the possible futures within God's plan.

The Nature of Prophecy: A Divine Connection to Time

Prophecy has long been seen as a window into **God's understanding of time**. In the Bible, prophets like Isaiah, Daniel, and John received visions of events to come, not because God was dictating every detail, but because **God exists beyond the limitations of time**. God can see each potential path and where each choice leads, understanding the vast spectrum of human decisions.

When Isaiah prophesied the coming of Jesus, he was tuned into a future moment as seen from God's timeless perspective. This didn't remove human choice from the equation; rather, it allowed humanity to prepare for a divine intervention that would alter the course of history.

Physics and the Many-Worlds Theory: A Scientific View of Possibilities

Modern physics offers us a fascinating perspective on the nature of time and possibilities. The **many-worlds interpretation** in quantum mechanics suggests that each decision or event creates a branching path, resulting in multiple possible futures. Just as prophecy envisions different potential outcomes, science shows us that time is full of possibilities, with each choice leading to a unique reality.

If **God is Time**, then perhaps prophecy reflects this vast landscape of choices and outcomes. When prophets speak of future events, they're not locked into one outcome but are instead glimpsing a path that aligns with divine will. These potential futures demonstrate that **time is not a rigid sequence but a flexible framework**, guided by both divine purpose and human choice.

Prophecy, Free Will, and the Role of Divine Timing

Prophecy isn't a fixed map; it's a blueprint that adapts to our choices. This means that while certain outcomes are foreseen, they're not inevitable. God, as Time, sees every possibility but allows humanity the freedom to choose its path. In this sense, prophecy serves as a **divine warning or encouragement**, guiding us toward choices that align with a higher purpose.

For example, in the Book of Jonah, God warned of Nineveh's destruction, but the people's decision to repent changed the outcome. This shows that **time's course isn't set in stone**; it's responsive, dynamic, and shaped by our interactions with the divine. When God reveals a prophecy, He's offering a glimpse of what could be, but it's up to humanity to determine if that path unfolds.

Time and the Unfolding of God's Plan

The Bible often speaks of events happening at an appointed time—moments that God has set aside to fulfill certain parts of His plan. Jesus' birth, for instance, happened when "the fullness of time had come." God's timing in prophecy is never random; it's perfectly chosen, as each event occurs to guide humanity closer to redemption.

From a human perspective, it may seem that time simply moves forward, but from God's perspective, **time is a tapestry**, weaving together past, present, and future. Prophecy serves as a thread in this divine tapestry, a hint at what God is working toward, but it's not absolute. As Time, God allows for an unfolding plan that takes into account every human action, every choice, and every prayer.

Prophecy and Spiritual Guidance

Prophecy can also serve as spiritual encouragement, offering hope and reassurance. The promise of a new earth, a place without suffering or pain, is a prophecy that aligns with God's ultimate desire for good. By sharing glimpses of this future, God invites us to live in ways that align with this vision. It's a call to **embrace goodness, to choose kindness, and to live with hope**.

Through prophecy, God as Time extends a hand, allowing us to participate in shaping the world we want to see. When we act in ways that reflect divine love, we move one step closer to fulfilling this ultimate vision. Prophecy reminds us that we are **partners with God in shaping our future**.

Reflective Prompts

- **Consider a time when you felt guided toward a specific choice.** Could this be a form of prophecy in your life, a glimpse of a future path?

- **Reflect on how free will and prophecy coexist.** How does knowing that you shape your future alongside God's plan change your approach to decision-making?

- **Think about the promises of hope in the Bible.** How might these prophetic messages guide you toward a more meaningful and intentional life

Chapter 8: The Eternal Kingdom – Beyond Time and Into Eternity

"Time is a sort of river of passing events, and strong is its current; no sooner is a thing brought to sight than it is swept by and another takes its place." – Marcus Aurelius

Imagine life as a river. Every day, you're standing on the bank, watching moments drift by—events, people, places, each one appearing and then slipping downstream. Life keeps moving forward, and the current doesn't stop for anyone. Yet, there's something we sense just beyond the horizon, a place where time itself might flow into something larger—something unchanging, maybe even eternal. **What if this is what the Bible means by an "eternal kingdom"?**

When we talk about eternity, we're talking about a place that goes beyond time. It's the **destination of all of this**, the grand finale where Time, Matter, and Space—the elements of the Trinity—finally settle into their ultimate roles. God, in this view, isn't just a spectator of the flow; God is the river and the ocean it flows into.

Eternity: A Place Beyond Time's Limits

In the Book of Revelation, we're given glimpses of this eternal place, where "God will wipe away every tear" and "there will be no more death or mourning or crying or pain." That's an incredible promise—a future where the struggles we face today won't even exist. But this isn't just about some far-off dream; it's about what God is leading us toward, step by step, through time.

If God is Time, then this eternal kingdom is **God's true nature**, where everything comes to rest. Imagine no more deadlines, no aging, no "before" or "after." It's a place where all the limitations we know are finally lifted, and we're left with the presence of God itself—an endless, unchanging now.

Is Timelessness Possible?

Believe it or not, science flirts with the idea of timelessness. Some physicists think that time might just be something our brains create to make sense of things, like a mental framework for stringing moments together. At the level of subatomic particles, time doesn't always behave the way we expect, suggesting that **time might be flexible or even optional** in certain realms of existence.

So if God is beyond time, maybe eternity is a dimension we can't quite wrap our heads around yet—a place where we're freed from time's rules. Imagine life like a river again, only this time, it flows into an ocean so vast that "before" and "after" become meaningless. This is the kingdom God speaks of—one that's waiting beyond our current horizon.

Redemption and the Eternal Kingdom

Redemption is a big part of this picture. Throughout the Bible, God's been moving humanity toward a place where everything broken is made whole. We're all part of this journey, moving through the river of time with purpose. The Bible says God will make "all things new," creating a new earth where suffering and injustice are finally over.

In this final vision, the roles of Time, Matter, and Space are completed. **God as Time** becomes an eternal presence that simply is, no longer bound to a timeline. **Jesus as Matter** isn't subject to decay, symbolizing life that's everlasting. And **the Holy Spirit as Space** fills every corner, connecting all things in a bond of peace. In this way, eternity isn't some "other place"; it's the ultimate goa where the Trinity's work finds its fulfillment.

How Do We Relate to Eternity?

Let's be honest—eternity is a hard thing to think about. Our lives revolve around time, schedules, and deadlines, so the idea of a "forever" can feel both comforting and intimidating. But eternity isn't just about living forever; it's about living fully, without fear or limitation. Imagine all the moments you've had that felt sacred or timeless—those glimpses are hints of the eternity that's coming.

And this isn't just about someday in the future. The vision of eternity changes how we live now. It gives us hope that every choice, every act of kindness, every time we choose compassion over judgment, contributes to this eternal kingdom. We're already part of it, moving closer with every decision we make that aligns us with God's love and purpose.

The Fulfillment of Time, Matter, and Space

In the eternal kingdom, everything comes together. **God as Time** becomes timeless; **Jesus as Matter** becomes everlasting; **the Holy Spirit as Space** becomes the full and final connection. This is where the Trinity's purpose is realized, where every element of existence reaches its highest state of being. In this place, time isn't just a river; it's the ocean that holds everything, all at once.

The eternal kingdom represents the end and the beginning, the point where all things align and where we find ourselves finally, truly home.

Reflective Prompts

- **Consider what a timeless existence might feel like.** How does imagining a world beyond time and change affect your view of life's challenges?

- **Reflect on the idea of eternity as a place of fulfillment.** How does the vision of an eternal kingdom inspire hope and purpose in your current life?

- **Think about the ultimate roles of Time, Matter, and Space in this eternal kingdom.** How might the Trinity's fulfillment shape your understanding of God's plan?

Chapter 9: Scientific and Philosophical Implications – Exploring the Divine in Reality

"What then is time? If no one asks me, I know what it is. If I wish to explain it to him who asks, I do not know." – St. Augustine

Time, space, and matter: These elements create the foundation of reality as we know it. We experience them daily, yet when we try to define them, they slip through our fingers like sand. This chapter explores these mysteries through the lenses of **science, philosophy, and spirituality**, diving into concepts that make us question everything we thought we knew about existence. What if these aren't just physical properties, but reflections of something deeper—something divine?

The Mysteries of Time in Physics and Philosophy

Time is one of the most fundamental yet mysterious aspects of reality. Physics tells us that time is not absolute; it's something that can be stretched, compressed, even reversed. **Einstein's theory of relativity** showed us that time is intimately connected to space, bending and warping around massive objects like planets and stars. Time is flexible, elastic, even subjective depending on where we are in the universe. This raises the question: **Is time merely a construct, or is it a glimpse into something eternal?**

Philosophers like Augustine and Kant saw time as both deeply personal and almost unknowable—a concept that defines our lives yet defies simple explanation. **Time, in a spiritual sense,** could be seen as the thread that connects us to the divine, an unseen but essential force that moves us forward, guiding us toward meaning and purpose.

The Role of Space: A Canvas for Existence

Space isn't just empty distance; it's the vast canvas on which reality unfolds. In **astrology**, space and celestial bodies play a role in shaping personality, timing, and fate. While some see astrology as symbolic, it reflects a deep intuition that **we are connected to the cosmos**. The movements of stars, planets, and galaxies influence life on Earth, suggesting that space isn't separate from us—it's a part of us, a field that holds potential and meaning.

In science, **quantum physics** reveals that space itself is not empty but filled with a "quantum foam" of particles popping in and out of existence. This hidden energy suggests that what we call "space" is teeming with possibility. Spiritually, space can be thought of as the **field of potential** in our lives, the infinite backdrop that holds every choice, every interaction, and every path we could take.

Matter as the Foundation of Transformation

Matter—the tangible, physical substance of existence—is constantly changing. Science shows us that **matter can neither be created nor destroyed**; it only changes forms. This brings a comforting thought: nothing is ever truly lost; it simply transforms. Spiritually, this idea reflects the **journey of the soul**, moving through phases of growth, loss, and renewal.

Matter is the vehicle through which we experience life, and each physical transformation hints at the potential for inner transformation. The **atoms in our bodies were once part of stars**, illustrating that matter, like us, is on a journey. We are physically connected to the universe, formed from the remnants of ancient stars, making our existence a cosmic miracle.

Spiritual Reflections: Finding Purpose in Time, Space, and Matter

If time, space, and matter are more than physical properties—if they are reflections of something divine—then how do they guide us spiritually? **Time becomes a teacher**, reminding us to cherish moments, to forgive, to grow, to seek purpose. **Space invites us to open up**, to explore possibilities, and to connect with others in meaningful ways. **Matter encourages transformation**, urging us to embrace change, to let go of what no longer serves us, and to become the people we are meant to be.

In this view, we aren't just passive observers of time, space, and matter; we are participants, co-creators with the universe, shaping reality through our actions, thoughts, and choices.

Beyond the Physical: The Divine Blueprint of Existence

The deeper we explore these elements, the more they seem to point toward a larger design—a divine blueprint that holds everything together. The universe, with its intricate balance of forces, its vast reaches of space, and its endless flow of time, suggests an intelligence, a guiding hand that has set everything in motion.

Imagine a cosmic architect, designing a universe where every atom, every star, every moment is part of a greater whole. Time, space, and matter are like the brushstrokes on this canvas, each one essential to the masterpiece. By understanding these elements as sacred, we start to see our lives not as random occurrences but as part of a **divine framework** that's always guiding us toward a greater purpose.

Reflections for a Meaningful Life

1. **How does seeing time as a teacher change your approach to life?** Consider the ways that time has shaped you, guided you, and allowed you to grow.

2. **What possibilities are you holding in your life's "space"?** Reflect on the potential for connection, growth, and discovery that surrounds you.

3. **In what ways have you experienced transformation?** Think about how change has played a role in your journey, much like matter transforming into new forms.

Chapter 10: Living Within the Mystery – Embracing the Unknown

"The past, like the future, is indefinite and exists only as a spectrum of possibilities." – Stephen Hawking

Have you ever found yourself at a crossroads, wondering what one decision might mean for your life? It's a feeling we all know. The choices we make every day, big or small, set us on different paths. Yet, when we think about the future, it's easy to imagine it as one straight line. But as Stephen Hawking suggested, **the future isn't a single path**; it's more like a web of potential outcomes, each decision creating a new branch.

Quantum theory shows us that particles exist in states of potential until they're observed, which means that **reality itself is shaped by what happens moment by moment**. If life is a spectrum of possibilities, then every choice, every action, every moment is like taking one thread of that web and giving it life. In this way, we're not just passengers in our lives; we're active participants, weaving our own unique story within a tapestry of endless possibilities.

The Web of Choices: Creating Our Own Timeline

Imagine your life as a branching tree, each decision taking you down a new path. The big choices—where to live, who to love, what dreams to pursue—are like major branches, setting the overall direction of your life. But even the smaller decisions, like how you spend your morning or how you treat someone, add new branches to that tree. **Every decision creates a ripple**, influencing not only our own future but the future of those around us.

This idea goes hand in hand with the quantum concept of **superposition**, where particles exist in multiple states until one state is chosen. Spiritually, this reflects the choices we make; each one brings us closer to one possible future and moves us away from another. In this way, the choices we make daily are powerful, weaving a reality that is constantly evolving.

Embracing the Unknown: The Adventure of Not Knowing

The fact that the future is open, waiting to be shaped, can be daunting—but it can also be thrilling. Rather than seeing life as a single path that we're stuck on, we can approach it as an adventure, a canvas with infinite potential. **Mystery invites us to live more fully**, to realize that we don't need to have all the answers to make meaningful choices. Embracing the unknown allows us to be present, to appreciate the unfolding moment, and to let go of the need for certainty.

Spiritually, embracing the unknown means letting go of the illusion of control. It's the ability to stand at the edge of a new day and accept that, no matter how much we plan, life is ultimately a blend of intention and unpredictability. Living within the mystery is about finding the balance between **making choices** and **allowing life to surprise us**.

The Interplay Between Science and Spirituality

Science has its own way of embracing the unknown. Every discovery leads to new questions, and many theories remain just that—possibilities, glimpses of what could be. Theories of **dark matter, dark energy, and quantum entanglement** reveal that reality is complex, with mysteries we can't fully grasp. But these unknowns don't stop us from exploring; they drive us to look deeper, to expand our understanding.

Spiritually, the unknown is much the same. We don't have all the answers, but that doesn't mean we stop searching. We live in a universe filled with possibilities, where every day presents new choices, new connections, new ways of seeing the world. In this way, both science and spirituality celebrate the mystery, encouraging us to live with curiosity and openness.

Living as Co-Creators with the Universe

If we're living in a web of possibilities, then we're not just observers—we're co-creators. The choices we make ripple outward, shaping our own lives and the lives of others. Think of it this way: every kind act, every moment of courage, every time we choose love over fear, we're adding positive energy to the web of reality. We're creating a life that aligns with the best possible version of ourselves.

This doesn't mean we'll always know the right path or make perfect decisions. But it does mean we have the power to shape our own story, to live with intention, and to embrace the idea that life is a collaborative process. **The universe provides the raw material, but we provide the vision**.

Reflective Prompts

1. **What possibilities exist in your life right now?** Think about the different paths open to you and how each one could create a unique future.

2. **How can you live with curiosity rather than seeking certainty?** Consider how a sense of wonder can change your experience of the unknown.

3. **Reflect on how your choices shape the lives of others.** What kind of future are you creating with the energy, actions, and intentions you bring into the world?

Chapter 11: The Cosmic Connection – Living as Part of the Universe

"We are not isolated from the cosmos; rather, we are woven into its fabric."

Think of the last time you felt truly connected to something bigger than yourself. Maybe it was during a walk in nature, a deep conversation, or simply watching the stars. That feeling of interconnectedness isn't just an emotion; it's a reminder that we are part of something vast and incredible—a cosmos that is alive with energy, possibilities, and meaning.

In this chapter, we explore what it means to see ourselves not as separate beings, but as part of the universe's intricate web. We're not bystanders in this cosmic journey; we're participants, influenced by everything around us and, in turn, influencing the universe through our actions, thoughts, and energy.

We Are Stardust: Our Cosmic Origins

One of the most profound scientific discoveries is that **we are literally made of stardust**. The elements in our bodies—carbon, nitrogen, oxygen, iron—all originated in stars that lived and died billions of years ago. Every atom within us is a piece of the universe's history, a product of cosmic events that stretch back to the beginning of time.

This means that **we're intrinsically connected to everything in the cosmos**. It's not just a metaphor; it's a physical truth. Each of us is a unique arrangement of particles that have traveled through time and space, forming and reforming as part of different beings, planets, even stars. Knowing this, we can see ourselves not as isolated individuals but as expressions of the universe's continuous journey.

The Spiritual Energy of Connection

If science shows us that we're physically connected to the universe, spirituality shows us that we're connected in ways that go beyond the physical. Many traditions speak of a universal energy, an underlying force that connects all things. Whether we call it the divine, the life force, or simply connection, this energy is what binds us to each other and to everything in existence.

Living with this awareness can transform how we see ourselves and others. Every interaction, every moment becomes part of a greater whole. Our actions ripple outward, touching the lives of people we may never meet. **When we act with kindness, compassion, or love**, we're adding positive energy to this universal field, contributing to the well-being of the entire cosmos.

Interconnectedness in Science and Nature

In nature, everything is interconnected. Ecosystems rely on a delicate balance where each organism, from the smallest bacteria to the largest trees, plays a role. The butterfly effect, a concept from chaos theory, suggests that **small changes can have far-reaching impacts**. A single action, like the flap of a butterfly's wings, can set off a chain reaction that influences weather patterns across the globe.

This concept reminds us that **we, too, have influence**. Every choice we make, every thought we entertain, creates ripples. When we see ourselves as connected to the universe in this way, our lives gain a deeper sense of purpose. Even our smallest actions contribute to the fabric of reality, like threads woven into a larger tapestry.

Living as Co-Creators with the Universe

Embracing our cosmic connection means recognizing that we're not passive observers of the universe; we're co-creators. Just as the universe has given us life, we have the power to shape our experiences, to influence the lives of others, and to leave our mark on the world.

This role of co-creator isn't about control; it's about participation. It's about understanding that **we're part of a dynamic, evolving process**, and that every choice we make contributes to the whole. Our thoughts, words, and actions create energy that flows into the universe, impacting the world around us. Living with this awareness encourages us to act intentionally, to bring positivity, creativity, and love into everything we do.

Finding Purpose in the Cosmic Dance

If we're part of a cosmic journey, then each of us has a unique role to play. We may not always understand how our actions fit into the larger picture, but that's part of the beauty of living within the mystery. Finding purpose doesn't mean finding all the answers; it means embracing the idea that **our lives matter**, that our actions have meaning, and that we're part of something incredible.

Every experience, every relationship, every moment is an opportunity to engage with this cosmic dance. Rather than seeing ourselves as separate, we can see ourselves as dancers, moving in harmony with the universe. Our purpose isn't something outside of us; it's woven into every interaction, every breath, every choice we make.

Reflections for Cosmic Living

1. **How do you feel connected to the universe?**
   Think about moments when you felt a deep
   sense of connection and what that means to you.

2. **Consider the impact of your actions.** How can
   you live in a way that adds positive energy to
   the world?

3. **Reflect on your purpose within the cosmic
   journey.** What unique gifts, passions, or
   perspectives can you bring to the world?

Chapter 12: Aligning with the Universe – Living with Purpose and Intention

"In every walk with nature one receives far more than he seeks." – John Muir

Imagine the feeling of being in perfect sync with the world around you. Maybe it's that rare day when everything seems to go right, when you feel at peace, energized, and connected. This feeling isn't just a coincidence—it's a sign of alignment, a state where we're in harmony with our surroundings, our purpose, and the universe itself.

In this chapter, we explore what it means to live in alignment with the universe. It's about tuning in to something deeper, letting go of resistance, and embracing the flow of life. When we align with the universe, we're not fighting against the current; we're moving with it, creating a life that feels meaningful, intentional, and connected.

Listening to Inner Wisdom: The Compass Within

Living in alignment begins with listening. We often look for answers outside of ourselves, but true alignment comes from within. Think of your intuition as a compass, a quiet but persistent voice that guides you toward choices that resonate with your true self. When we ignore this inner wisdom, life can feel chaotic and disconnected. But when we listen, we're more likely to find paths that bring us joy, peace, and fulfillment.

Spiritual alignment means tuning into that inner voice and trusting it, even when it doesn't make logical sense. This is the universe's way of guiding us, gently nudging us toward paths that align with our unique purpose. It's a reminder that **our true path isn't something we need to force; it's something we discover by listening**.

Going with the Flow: Embracing Life's Rhythm

Life is full of ups and downs, unexpected turns, and changes in direction. When we try to control every detail, we often end up feeling frustrated, exhausted, and out of sync. But when we let go and allow life to unfold, we're better able to see the beauty in its rhythm. **Flowing with life's current** doesn't mean giving up on our goals; it means being open to change, adapting, and trusting that there's a purpose even in the unexpected.

Aligning with the universe means recognizing that we're part of a larger rhythm. We don't always have to know the destination; sometimes, we just need to trust the process. The more we embrace life's rhythm, the more we're able to see opportunities in challenges, growth in setbacks, and meaning in every moment.

Living with Intention: The Power of Purpose

Alignment isn't passive; it's active, intentional, and purposeful. Living with intention means being mindful of the energy we bring into each moment, the actions we take, and the words we speak. Every choice becomes a way of expressing who we are and what we stand for. When we live intentionally, we're not just drifting through life; we're actively participating in it, shaping our own experience and contributing to the world.

Imagine waking up each day with a sense of purpose, knowing that each action you take, each word you speak, aligns with your core values. This is what it means to live with intention. It's about creating a life that feels authentic, one where you're in harmony with the universe because you're fully aligned with yourself.

The Spiritual Practice of Alignment

Alignment with the universe isn't a one-time achievement; it's an ongoing practice. It requires mindfulness, reflection, and sometimes, a willingness to course-correct. Here are a few ways to cultivate this alignment:

- **Daily Reflection**: Spend a few moments each day asking yourself, "What feels right to me today?" This simple practice can help you stay connected to your intuition and align with choices that resonate.

- **Mindful Actions**: Approach each action with intention, from the way you interact with others to the energy you bring to your work. Small acts of mindfulness create a ripple effect that brings more alignment into every part of your life.

- **Letting Go of Resistance**: Notice where you feel resistance in life. Often, this resistance is a sign that something isn't in alignment. By letting go of resistance, we make space for what truly serves us, allowing life to flow more smoothly.

Connecting with the Universe through Nature

Nature offers us a beautiful example of alignment. When we observe the natural world, we see a harmony that flows effortlessly—the tides that follow the moon's pull, the trees that change with the seasons, the animals that move instinctively. By spending time in nature, we can reconnect with this rhythm, reminding ourselves that alignment doesn't have to be forced; it's a natural state.

Nature has a way of grounding us, of bringing us back to the present moment. When we feel lost or disconnected, stepping outside, breathing in fresh air, or watching a sunset can remind us that we, too, are part of this larger cycle. Just as the stars have their orbits and the rivers their paths, **we have our own path**, one that becomes clear when we allow ourselves to be present and open.

Reflections for an Aligned Life

1. **What does alignment feel like to you?** Reflect on times when you've felt at peace, purposeful, and connected, and think about what brought you there.

2. **How can you create more space for intuition in your life?** Consider practices that help you listen to your inner voice, like journaling, meditation, or simply slowing down.

3. **In what areas of your life can you live with more intention?** Identify specific actions or choices that would bring you into greater harmony with your values and purpose.

Chapter 13: The Power of Connection – Finding Meaning Through Relationships

"We are each other's harvest; we are each other's business; we are each other's magnitude and bond."
– Gwendolyn Brooks

Think about the people who feel like "home" to you—those rare connections where you just click, as if you've known them forever. We often think of soulmates as romantic partners, but what if soulmates come in all forms? A soulmate could be a friend, a family member, or even a teacher or mentor. These are people who bring out our truest selves, who feel like part of our life's purpose. The connection feels natural, almost inevitable, like some unseen force brought you together.

Just as forces in nature pull certain objects together, the universe seems to draw certain people into our lives. Some of these connections are like magnets—unexplainable yet undeniable. Others are steady, grounding influences, like atoms that bond to form something stable. By understanding these connections through the lens of science, we can appreciate the profound ways people shape our lives.

The Science of Attraction: Magnets, Atoms, and Gravity

Attraction isn't just a feeling; it's also a physical phenomenon. In nature, **magnetic forces, atomic bonds, and gravitational pull** create relationships between objects, pulling them together to form something greater. These natural forces mirror the ways we connect with certain people on a deep, unexplainable level.

- **Magnetism**: Just like magnets have opposite poles that pull them together, some people feel like they were meant to be in our lives. This "magnetic" connection can create an instant bond that feels both intense and natural.

Whether it's a friend, family member, or partner, this connection feels like two energies coming together in a way that can't be ignored.

- **Atomic Bonds**: Atoms bond with each other to create stability. Similarly, some relationships feel grounding and supportive, providing us with a sense of balance and security. These are often the friends, mentors, and loved ones who are constants in our lives, strengthening us by their presence.

- **Gravitational Pull**: Every object with mass exerts a gravitational pull, attracting other objects toward it. This pull is subtle, but it's there, becoming stronger the closer we are. Similarly, there are people who enter our lives slowly, but their influence grows over time. The more we connect, the stronger the bond becomes, much like gravity.

Each of these scientific forces can be seen as metaphors for human connection. Soulmates aren't limited to romantic partners—they can be anyone who feels like a natural part of our lives, as though some invisible force led us to them.

Soulmates Beyond Romance

The idea of a soulmate isn't limited to love interests. Some soulmates are friends who understand us in ways few others do, while others may be family members whose bond feels deeply spiritual. These people don't complete us but complement us, bringing out our best qualities and helping us grow.

Friendship soulmates, for example, might share our passions, dreams, or even our struggles. They're the people we can call in the middle of the night, who listen without judgment, and who seem to understand us even without words. Family soulmates may be siblings or even a parent or child with whom we feel an especially strong connection—a sense of purpose that goes beyond biology.

These relationships remind us that **soulmates are part of our soul's journey**. They come into our lives to teach us, to support us, and to help us become who we're meant to be.

Connections as Catalysts for Growth

Relationships that feel "meant to be" often act as catalysts, challenging us and pushing us forward. Just as certain molecules bond to form something entirely new, our relationships can create change, transformation, and growth. Soulmate connections, whether romantic, platonic, or familial, help us see ourselves more clearly. They act as mirrors, showing us both our strengths and our weaknesses, encouraging us to grow.

Sometimes these connections are comfortable and nurturing; other times, they're intense and challenging. But each one plays a role in our personal journey, helping us reach our fullest potential. These people bring out parts of ourselves that we may not even know are there, just as magnets reveal hidden magnetic fields or atoms bond to create new elements.

Embracing the Mystery of Soul Connections

Not every connection can be explained logically. Some people come into our lives with a sense of purpose that we can't quite put into words. This is where we can embrace the mystery, acknowledging that not everything needs to be understood. Soul connections remind us that **life is a balance of intention and serendipity**, a dance between choice and destiny.

When we encounter a soulmate, it can feel like the universe aligning, like everything makes sense in a way it didn't before. These relationships may last a lifetime, or they may be brief but impactful. Either way, they leave an imprint on our lives, shaping who we are and who we're becoming.

Reflections on Connection and Soulmates

1. **Who are the soulmates in your life?** Think about people who bring meaning, growth, and a sense of purpose to your journey, whether they're friends, family, or even mentors.

2. **Consider the bonds you feel with certain people.** Reflect on how different connections have acted as mirrors, showing you aspects of yourself you may not have seen otherwise.

3. **How do you nurture these profound connections?** Consider ways to honor these relationships, bringing mindfulness, gratitude, and authenticity to your interactions.

Chapter 14: The Inner Journey – Discovering Purpose and Growth

"Knowing yourself is the beginning of all wisdom."
– Aristotle

Imagine each choice as a step on a branching path. Some choices lead us closer to a life filled with purpose, growth, and fulfillment, while others may take us in directions that feel limiting or unaligned with who we truly are. Self-discovery is a compass that helps us navigate these timelines, showing us how to make choices that lead to a more meaningful, positive life. When we know ourselves—our values, strengths, and dreams—we can better align with the path that brings us closer to our fullest potential.

Each decision we make has the power to put us on a different timeline. Some paths will offer lessons and challenges, while others may lead to deeper connections and new opportunities. This chapter explores how **self-awareness and intentional choices** can shape the timeline of our lives, guiding us toward growth and purpose

Reflection as a Guide to Choosing the Right Path

Reflection helps us understand where we've been, where we're headed, and how we might want to change course. Think of reflection as a map that shows us both the positive and negative patterns in our lives. When we reflect, we recognize the moments when we felt aligned and at peace, as well as the times when we may have felt lost or disconnected.

Every choice has the potential to shift our timeline. Reflection helps us choose with intention, showing us which decisions will lead to positive growth and which might set us back. By regularly reflecting, we can course-correct, making small adjustments that lead us closer to our ideal timeline—one filled with purpose, alignment, and peace.

Choosing Growth: The Impact of Small Decisions

Sometimes, growth doesn't come from a single big decision but from a series of small, intentional choices. Each moment we choose kindness, patience, or courage, we're steering our lives in a positive direction. Even small decisions, like how we respond to challenges or how we treat ourselves and others, have a ripple effect that can alter our timeline.

Imagine your life as a garden. Each choice is a seed you plant, shaping the future landscape of your life. Positive choices plant seeds of growth, compassion, and resilience, creating a timeline that's filled with beauty and purpose. Negative choices, on the other hand, can lead to a tangled, overgrown path that feels chaotic or limiting. By choosing growth, we're planting seeds that lead us toward a timeline of fulfillment and positivity.

The Role of Vulnerability in Choosing Our Path

Vulnerability is a powerful force in shaping our lives. When we allow ourselves to be vulnerable, we open up to growth, connection, and self-understanding. It takes courage to admit when we're unsure or when we've made mistakes, but vulnerability also creates space for healing and change.

Choosing to embrace vulnerability can lead us down a timeline filled with authentic relationships and personal growth. It's the willingness to be open and honest with ourselves and others that allows us to evolve. Vulnerability may feel uncomfortable, but it's often the key to aligning with a positive, growth-filled timeline.

Parallel Timelines: The Potential Paths We Could Take

Each choice we make has the potential to create a parallel timeline—a version of our life that plays out differently based on our decisions. The idea of parallel timelines suggests that there are many possible versions of our lives, each shaped by our choices. When we choose growth, compassion, or courage, we move toward a timeline that's aligned with our true potential.

Imagine standing at a crossroads. Each path represents a different version of your life, a timeline shaped by the choices you make. Some paths may be filled with positive experiences, growth, and fulfillment, while others may feel challenging or unaligned. By choosing with intention, we're not only shaping our current life but also creating a future that's more aligned with who we want to become.

Embracing Change as Part of the Journey

Growth isn't a straight line; it's a winding path with unexpected turns, setbacks, and moments of transformation. Each twist and turn represents a choice, an opportunity to grow or to retreat. Change is part of life, and it's through change that we often find our greatest lessons. Embracing change as part of the journey allows us to adapt, to learn, and to continue growing, even when the path is uncertain.

By choosing to embrace change, we're opening ourselves up to new timelines, new possibilities, and new versions of ourselves. Change can feel uncomfortable, but it's also a chance to realign, to move closer to a life that feels meaningful and true.

Reflection Prompts for Embracing Timelines and Growth

1. **What choices have shaped your life?** Reflect on moments when you made decisions that led to growth or change, and consider how those choices shaped your current path.

2. **What timeline do you want to create?** Think about the future you envision and the choices you can make to move toward that reality.

3. **How can you embrace growth in your everyday decisions?** Consider the small ways you can choose growth, compassion, and courage, knowing that each choice shapes your journey.

Chapter 15: The Sacredness of Presence – Being Fully in the Moment

"Time present and time past are both perhaps present in time future, and time future contained in time past." – T.S. Eliot

Imagine a moment so full it feels timeless. Maybe it's the laughter of a loved one, the stillness of a sunrise, or the simple feeling of contentment in your own space. Moments like these feel as if they hold an eternity within them, as if the past, present, and future are all wrapped up into one. This is the power of presence—an awareness that goes beyond just "being here." It's about immersing ourselves fully in the now, recognizing it as sacred, and experiencing life with a sense of wonder and gratitude.

The past shapes us, the future calls us, but the present is where we truly live. This chapter explores how embracing presence can transform our lives, helping us see each moment as a sacred part of our journey.

The Art of Being Here Now

It's easy to feel caught between regrets of the past and worries about the future. Our minds have a way of pulling us in different directions, distracting us from the beauty of the present. But when we practice presence, we give ourselves a gift—a moment of clarity, of peace, of connection with what is here right now. This can be as simple as taking a deep breath, feeling the ground beneath our feet, or really listening to the people around us.

Presence is the essence of mindfulness, a practice that encourages us to bring our full attention to whatever we're doing. When we're present, we're not just observing life; we're participating in it fully, experiencing each moment as if it's a work of art unfolding in real time.

The Timelessness Within Each Moment

Moments of true presence have a way of feeling timeless. Think of how time seems to slow down when you're deeply engaged—whether it's in a conversation, a creative pursuit, or simply watching the world go by. **These moments hold a timeless quality**, as if they exist outside of the usual flow of time, offering us a glimpse into something eternal.

When we're fully present, we transcend the usual limitations of time. The past doesn't pull us back, the future doesn't push us forward; instead, we're simply here, experiencing life in its purest form. In these moments, we're reminded that each second holds its own beauty, its own value. Presence allows us to tap into this timelessness, giving us a sense of peace that goes beyond our day-to-day concerns.

Presence as a Spiritual Practice

Being present isn't just a practice; it's a spiritual experience. When we're fully in the moment, we're opening ourselves to something greater than ourselves. We're acknowledging the divine within each experience, seeing each moment as part of a larger tapestry. This is why practices like meditation, mindful breathing, or even gratitude rituals are so powerful— they connect us with the sacredness of life.

Presence helps us cultivate a sense of gratitude for the "ordinary" moments. Rather than constantly seeking the next big thing, we can find contentment in what's right here. Whether it's a conversation with a friend, a quiet morning, or a meal shared with loved ones, presence allows us to see these moments for the gifts they truly are.

The Interplay of Past, Present, and Future

Just as T.S. Eliot suggests, time is interconnected; the past, present, and future influence one another. The experiences we've had in the past shape how we see the world, and our dreams for the future guide our actions today. Yet the present is where these two meet, where we can actively choose how to respond, how to move forward, and how to let go.

Living in the present doesn't mean ignoring the past or the future; it means honoring them by bringing our best selves into the current moment. When we acknowledge the impact of the past and keep our future goals in mind, we can make choices in the present that align with our deepest values and highest intentions.

Cultivating Presence in Everyday Life

Presence doesn't require grand gestures; it's something we can practice in small ways every day. Here are a few ways to cultivate presence and bring more peace into your life:

- **Mindful Breathing**: Simply taking a few deep breaths can bring you back to the present, helping you feel grounded and centered.

- **Gratitude Journaling**: Reflecting on what you're grateful for each day helps shift your focus to the positive aspects of the present moment.

- **Active Listening**: When you're with someone, practice truly listening, without distractions. This simple act brings you fully into the moment and strengthens your connection.

Reflections for a Life of Presence

1. **What moments make you feel fully present?**
   Think about experiences that bring you into the
   "now" and consider how you can bring more of
   these moments into your life.

2. **How can you practice gratitude in the
   present moment?** Reflect on ways to cultivate
   appreciation for the here and now.

3. **What can you let go of to live more fully in
   the present?** Consider any regrets or worries
   that may be pulling you away from the beauty
   of the current moment.

Chapter 16: Embracing Uncertainty – Finding Peace in the Unknown

"The past, like the future, is indefinite and exists only as a spectrum of possibilities." – Stephen Hawking

Life is full of questions without easy answers. What will happen tomorrow? How will our choices play out? The unknown can be unsettling, especially when we crave clarity and control. But what if uncertainty isn't something to fear? What if it's a doorway to possibility, a space where life's mysteries unfold? This chapter explores how embracing the unknown can lead to a life of openness, peace, and curiosity.

Living with uncertainty is a powerful way to expand beyond our comfort zones. When we stop needing every answer, we create space for new experiences and unexpected growth. **The unknown becomes a source of possibility**, a reminder that life is always shifting, and that we, too, can evolve with it.

Why We Fear the Unknown

As humans, we're wired to seek security and predictability. We like knowing what's next, feeling like we have control over our future. But the truth is, life rarely unfolds exactly as we plan. **The unknown is a constant presence**—an open field where anything can happen. Learning to embrace it means finding peace in that uncertainty, allowing it to coexist with our hopes and dreams.

When we fear the unknown, we limit ourselves to what feels safe. But in doing so, we may miss out on the richness that life has to offer. Embracing uncertainty isn't about letting go of goals or plans; it's about releasing the need for certainty. This mindset shift can transform fear into curiosity, turning the unknown into a field of potential rather than something to be avoided.

The Unknown as a Field of Possibility

Imagine the unknown as a blank canvas, waiting to be filled with color and shape. Just as Stephen Hawking described, the future exists as a spectrum of possibilities. When we approach life with this mindset, we see that the unknown is full of opportunities waiting to unfold. **Each moment is a brushstroke**, a chance to create something new, something we couldn't predict but might find beautiful.

Embracing this field of possibility requires faith—faith in ourselves, in the journey, and in the idea that life's mysteries hold value. When we stop trying to control every outcome, we find a greater freedom to explore, to learn, and to create a life that feels aligned with our deepest self.

Finding Purpose in the Journey, Not the Destination

When we're focused on knowing exactly where we're headed, we often lose sight of the journey itself. But **purpose isn't always about reaching a final destination**; it's about discovering meaning in every step we take. Embracing uncertainty invites us to find purpose in the process, to live with curiosity and openness rather than rigid expectations.

This approach allows us to be more adaptable, resilient, and open to life's twists and turns. Rather than feeling defeated when plans change, we can see change as a new path unfolding. Each unexpected turn becomes an opportunity to learn, to grow, and to find a deeper understanding of ourselves and our world.

The Role of Faith in Embracing the Unknown

Faith doesn't necessarily mean belief in something specific; it can be as simple as trust—trust in life, trust in ourselves, and trust in the journey. When we have faith, we allow ourselves to release the need for certainty, knowing that even if we don't have all the answers, we're still moving forward. Faith is a grounding force, giving us the strength to face uncertainty with courage and an open heart.

By cultivating faith, we build resilience, the ability to navigate life's ups and downs with a sense of inner peace. Faith allows us to approach the unknown not with fear, but with a calm curiosity, seeing each moment as an opportunity to experience something new.

Practical Ways to Embrace the Unknown

- **Stay Curious**: Curiosity transforms fear into exploration. When we approach the unknown with a mindset of discovery, we open ourselves up to new experiences and insights.

- **Practice Letting Go**: Embrace the things you can't control by focusing on what you can. This practice helps us release attachment to specific outcomes, making space for new possibilities.

- **Mindful Presence**: Ground yourself in the present moment rather than dwelling on future uncertainties. Presence reminds us that while the future is unknown, the current moment is a place of peace and possibility.

Reflections for Embracing the Unknown

1. **What areas of your life feel uncertain right now?** Reflect on how you can approach these areas with curiosity instead of fear.

2. **How can you cultivate faith in the journey?** Think about small practices, like mindfulness or gratitude, that help you release the need for certainty.

3. **Consider a past experience where uncertainty led to growth.** How did embracing the unknown open doors or bring unexpected wisdom?

Chapter 17: The Power of Imagination and Manifestation – Shaping Reality Through Thought

"Imagination is everything. It is the preview of life's coming attractions." – Albert Einstein

Think of your dreams as seeds. With a vision, intention, and a bit of faith, you plant them in the soil of possibility. Manifestation is the process of nurturing those seeds until they blossom into reality. It's about more than just dreaming; it's about using our imagination as a tool to guide our actions and intentions toward creating the life we envision.

This chapter explores the connection between imagination and manifestation, showing how our inner world influences our outer reality. **When we dream with purpose and intention, we're participating in the act of creation,** aligning our thoughts, beliefs, and actions to bring our visions to life.

Manifestation: Turning Dreams into Reality

Manifestation is rooted in the idea that our thoughts, beliefs, and intentions shape our reality. Just as **imagination allows us to see beyond the present moment**, manifestation allows us to bring those visions into our lived experience. But manifestation isn't just about thinking positive thoughts; it's about aligning our actions, intentions, and mindset with our goals.

In many spiritual teachings, the idea of manifestation reflects a principle that's echoed in the Bible: "As a man thinketh in his heart, so is he" (Proverbs 23:7). This verse highlights the power of belief, suggesting that our inner thoughts have the potential to shape who we become and what we experience.

Imagination as the First Step in Manifestation

Manifestation begins with imagination. When we vividly picture what we desire, we're sending a clear message to the universe—and to ourselves—about what we want. The mind doesn't always distinguish between a vividly imagined scenario and reality; this is why visualization is so powerful. **When we imagine, we create an internal roadmap** that guides our subconscious toward the life we want.

Picture your dreams as scenes playing out in your mind. Each time you visualize, you're reinforcing that mental image, making it more likely to materialize. This is a form of mental rehearsal, a way of "practicing" the life you want to live, preparing yourself to recognize opportunities that align with your vision.

Faith and Action: The Heart of Manifestation

Manifestation isn't just about believing; it's about pairing faith with action. **Faith without action is like planting a seed but never watering it.** Faith gives us the courage to pursue our dreams, to keep going even when we face obstacles. When we combine faith with intention, we're not just waiting for life to happen; we're actively participating in the creation of our own reality.

In Hebrews 11:1, faith is described as "the assurance of things hoped for, the conviction of things not seen." Manifestation requires a similar conviction—trusting that even though our dreams haven't yet materialized, they are real and attainable. This belief empowers us to take concrete steps toward our goals, to show up each day with the mindset that we're moving closer to what we desire.

Aligning Imagination, Intention, and Action

Manifestation is about alignment—aligning our imagination with our intentions, and aligning our intentions with our actions. When we set intentions, we're bringing focus and clarity to our desires, anchoring them in reality. This alignment creates momentum, moving us toward our dreams in practical, tangible ways.

Consider it like setting a destination on a GPS. Imagination is choosing the destination, intention is mapping the route, and action is taking the steps to get there. This process transforms our dreams from abstract thoughts into achievable goals, empowering us to create a reality that reflects our truest aspirations.

Manifestation in Daily Practice

Manifestation isn't a one-time effort; it's a daily practice that builds momentum over time. Here are some ways to incorporate manifestation into your everyday life:

- **Visualization**: Spend a few minutes each day visualizing your goals. Imagine yourself living the life you want, feeling the emotions, and experiencing the outcomes as if they're already real.

- **Setting Intentions**: Each morning, set an intention that aligns with your goals. Write it down, say it out loud, or hold it in your mind as a guiding principle for the day.

- **Gratitude for What's to Come**: Practice gratitude not only for what you have but for what you're creating. This "future gratitude" helps anchor your faith and reinforces your commitment to your vision.

Reflections on Imagination and Manifestation

1. **What do you envision for your future?**
    Reflect on your deepest dreams, and consider
    how you can make those visions more vivid and
    real in your imagination.

2. **How can you bring intention to your
    manifestations?** Think about ways to align your
    thoughts, actions, and mindset with the future
    you want to create.

3. **What steps can you take to turn your dreams
    into reality?** Consider small, intentional actions
    that bring you closer to manifesting your goals.

Chapter 18: Embracing Transformation – Growing Through Life's Changes

"The only way to make sense out of change is to plunge into it, move with it, and join the dance." – Alan Watts

Change is one of life's few certainties. Whether it's a new chapter, a sudden loss, a shift in perspective, or a leap of faith, transformation shapes us in ways we often can't foresee. Embracing transformation means allowing ourselves to evolve, to release what no longer serves us, and to open to what's yet to come. **Each transformation offers a fresh opportunity** to become more aligned with our truest self, more resilient, and more compassionate.

This chapter explores how change, though often uncomfortable, is essential for growth. It's about finding grace in the midst of transitions and trusting that transformation, however unexpected, has a purpose.

Transformation as a Lifelong Process

Transformation isn't a one-time event; it's a constant in life. Just as seasons change, we go through cycles of growth, shedding, and renewal. Some changes are small, like adjusting to a new routine, while others are life-altering, forcing us to redefine who we are. Transformation invites us to release outdated beliefs, embrace new truths, and continually become a more authentic version of ourselves.

Rather than resisting change, we can learn to view it as a teacher. **Every transformation is an opportunity to learn, to adapt, and to find meaning in new experiences.** Embracing transformation means seeing each change as part of our journey, a chapter in the story of who we're becoming.

The Power of Letting Go

One of the greatest challenges of transformation is letting go of what we've outgrown. Whether it's a relationship, a job, a habit, or even an old identity, letting go creates space for something new. Holding on too tightly can keep us stuck, but when we release, we allow ourselves to move forward.

Letting go requires courage and trust, especially when we're stepping into the unknown. **When we let go, we're not losing; we're making room for something that aligns better with who we are now.** By releasing what no longer serves us, we're honoring the process of growth and giving ourselves permission to change.

Transformation as a Spiritual Journey

Transformation often challenges us on a spiritual level. It can bring up questions about our purpose, our beliefs, and the nature of existence itself. This is especially true during major life changes, when we're forced to reassess what truly matters. Transformation invites us to look inward, to seek answers beyond the surface, and to find a sense of peace within ourselves.

In many spiritual traditions, transformation is seen as a path to enlightenment or self-realization. It's the process of shedding layers, revealing our true essence, and moving closer to a deeper understanding of ourselves and the universe. Each transformation, however challenging, brings us closer to our most authentic self, teaching us resilience, humility, and compassion.

Finding Strength in Vulnerability

Transformation often brings vulnerability. When we're going through a major change, it's normal to feel uncertain, emotional, or even lost. But vulnerability is a source of strength; it's what allows us to connect with others, to ask for help, and to grow. Vulnerability isn't a weakness; it's a sign of courage—a willingness to be open, to trust, and to embrace the unknown.

By allowing ourselves to be vulnerable, we open up to support, insight, and new perspectives. Vulnerability creates space for healing, helping us navigate transformation with grace and resilience. **When we're willing to be vulnerable, we're embracing transformation as an opportunity for growth** rather than something to fear.

Living in Alignment with Change

To embrace transformation is to live in alignment with the rhythm of life. Change is part of nature, part of the universe's constant flow. Just as trees shed their leaves and rivers carve new paths, we're meant to evolve, to adapt, and to grow. **When we embrace change, we're participating in the dance of life**, moving in harmony with the universe's cycles of growth and renewal.

Living in alignment with change doesn't mean we won't feel discomfort; it means we accept that discomfort as part of the journey. Each transformation brings its own lessons, and by leaning into change, we discover the resilience, creativity, and courage within us.

Reflections for Embracing Transformation

1. **What changes are you currently experiencing?** Reflect on how these changes are challenging or inspiring you and what lessons they might be bringing.

2. **How can you let go of what no longer serves you?** Consider any beliefs, habits, or attachments that may be holding you back from fully embracing transformation.

3. **In what ways can vulnerability guide your growth?** Think about how being open, both with yourself and others, can help you navigate change with grace.

Chapter 19: Time as the Path of Redemption – Understanding Growth Through Divine Time

"Time is the number of movement in respect of before and after." – Aristotle

Consider the way time shapes our lives. It carries us forward, allowing us to learn, to heal, and to grow. In this sense, time itself becomes a tool of transformation, a pathway that guides us toward redemption and renewal. When we view time as more than hours on a clock—as something sacred, as the presence of God— each moment becomes a step on a divine path that ultimately leads us closer to truth, love, and self-understanding.

This chapter explores how time, seen as a force of God, creates opportunities for redemption and growth. From a scientific perspective, time gives structure to change. Spiritually, time allows for repentance, healing, and the unfolding of purpose. When we align with this view of time, we see life not as a series of isolated moments but as a meaningful journey.

Time as the Engine of Redemption

In the Bible, time is often portrayed as a force through which God works His purpose. Consider the phrase from Ecclesiastes, "For everything there is a season, and a time for every matter under heaven" (Ecclesiastes 3:1). This view sees time as a divine tool, a method through which life's cycles of growth, rest, and transformation unfold. In this context, **time becomes a sacred passage** through which we're constantly invited to renew and redeem ourselves.

From a spiritual perspective, time offers us chances to reflect, repent, and start anew. Redemption isn't a single event; it's a process that unfolds with each moment, each decision, each step forward. By embracing time as God's presence in our lives, we allow ourselves to see each experience—even the challenging ones—as part of a divine plan for growth.

The Science of Time and Transformation

In physics, time is essential to understanding motion and change. Without time, there is no before or after, no cause and effect. **Time is the element that gives structure to transformation**. Astrophysics shows us that even galaxies evolve over billions of years, their shapes and movements governed by the passage of cosmic time. This slow but constant change is mirrored in our own lives, where personal growth and transformation unfold gradually, often in unseen ways.

On an atomic level, matter itself is constantly in flux. Particles shift, bond, and release, continually shaping new forms. This ongoing process of change suggests that time is an underlying force in all creation—a force that allows for the emergence of new possibilities, new structures, and new life. **In the same way, time allows us to grow and transform**, giving us the opportunity to become more than we were yesterday.

Astrological Time and Life Cycles

Astrology views time as cyclical, marked by repeating patterns that influence our experiences. Just as planets follow orbits, creating cycles of growth, challenge, and renewal, so do we follow cycles of transformation. Each phase offers us a chance to revisit themes, heal wounds, and evolve. In astrology, time is seen as both personal and universal, shaping our lives through meaningful cycles.

When we view time this way, we start to see patterns in our lives that mirror cosmic rhythms. We may experience recurring challenges that invite us to grow or patterns of healing that guide us toward redemption. Just as the planets move predictably, returning to similar positions across time, we're given repeated opportunities to evolve, to choose love over fear, and to embrace our higher selves.

Redemption Through Time: A Spiritual Journey

When we align with the divine view of time, we understand that **redemption is a journey rather than a destination**. We're given moments of grace, moments where time pauses and allows us to see clearly, to make choices that align with love, forgiveness, and compassion. Redemption unfolds as we live in the presence of God as time, walking through experiences that shape and refine us.

The Bible speaks of God's plan unfolding "in the fullness of time," a reminder that certain events, transformations, and blessings come when the time is right. Just as fruit ripens at the proper season, our own growth and redemption arrive according to divine timing. This perspective brings comfort, helping us trust that every step, every challenge, and every joy is part of a greater plan.

Living in Harmony with Divine Time

To live in harmony with divine time means trusting the process of growth and redemption. It means accepting that our journey will have seasons of light and darkness, of joy and struggle. When we understand that time is sacred, we're more willing to let go of impatience and embrace each moment for what it brings.

Divine time teaches us patience, a virtue that allows us to wait with faith. We learn to trust that even the waiting periods have purpose, that the unfolding of life's events isn't random but part of a carefully woven plan. Each phase of time—whether painful or joyful— becomes a chapter in our personal story of redemption, one that leads us closer to God's ultimate design.

Reflections for Embracing Divine Time

1. **What areas of your life feel like they're "in process"?** Reflect on ways to embrace these as part of a larger journey of growth and redemption.

2. **How can you align with the divine rhythm of time?** Consider ways to practice patience, trust, and acceptance of life's timing.

3. **Think about how time has shaped your journey of redemption.** Reflect on moments where you've experienced growth, healing, or forgiveness over time.

Chapter 20: The Eternal Soul – Beyond Time and the Journey of Existence

"The soul that is within me no man can degrade." –
Frederick Douglass

What if time is not just something we move through, but something our souls transcend? In many spiritual traditions, the soul is seen as eternal, a spark of divinity that exists beyond the constraints of time and space. If time is an expression of God, then perhaps the soul, too, is an extension of that divine essence. The soul's journey, shaped by the events of each life, each moment, isn't bound by a single lifetime; it's part of a continuous, unfolding story.

This chapter explores the eternal nature of the soul, its connection to the divine, and the ways in which the soul's journey might unfold beyond the bounds of earthly time. Science and philosophy both offer intriguing hints about this concept, aligning with spiritual views that our lives are not isolated; rather, they're interconnected, part of a greater, timeless whole.

The Timeless Soul and Spiritual Perspectives

In spiritual traditions, the soul is often seen as a piece of eternity. In the Bible, Ecclesiastes speaks to this idea: "He has made everything beautiful in its time. He has also set eternity in the human heart" (Ecclesiastes 3:11). This passage suggests that we carry eternity within us— a timeless connection to the divine.

Religions and philosophies across cultures have recognized the soul's continuity, seeing it as something that lives on, experiencing, learning, and evolving through various forms. The concept of reincarnation in Eastern spirituality and the Christian notion of an afterlife both reflect the belief that the soul transcends the physical limits of time. The soul's journey could be viewed as one that stretches across lifetimes, each one contributing to the soul's ultimate growth and understanding.

Scientific Insights and the Mystery of Consciousness

The nature of consciousness—the essence of what makes us who we are—remains one of science's greatest mysteries. While the brain is a biological organ, consciousness itself defies easy explanation. Some physicists and neuroscientists have even speculated that **consciousness may not be fully confined to the brain**; instead, it may be connected to something larger, potentially existing beyond the physical.

Quantum theory hints at the possibility of consciousness interacting with the universe in ways we don't yet understand. If we consider consciousness as a form of energy—something that can neither be created nor destroyed—it opens up the idea that **our consciousness, our soul, might continue in some form** even after the physical body ceases to exist. This aligns with the concept of an eternal soul, one that transcends physical existence.

Philosophy and the Continuity of Self

Philosophers have long debated the nature of the self and its continuity beyond physical life. Plato wrote about the soul's eternal journey, suggesting that each life is a step in the process of self-realization. He saw life as a cycle in which the soul seeks knowledge, wisdom, and ultimately, unity with the divine.

Modern philosophy has also explored the idea of identity and existence beyond physical boundaries. Existentialist thought, while often focused on the tangible experience of life, leaves room for the mystery of consciousness and the possibility that our essence is part of something greater. **Our experiences, actions, and relationships create ripples** that extend beyond our immediate surroundings, impacting the lives of others in ways that may outlast our physical selves.

The Soul's Journey as a Reflection of Divine Time

If God is time, then our souls are expressions of that divine presence, moving through experiences that shape and refine us. Time becomes the canvas on which the soul's journey unfolds. This view helps us see each moment, each lifetime, as part of a greater story, one in which **the soul continues to evolve, learn, and return to its divine source**.

In this way, time isn't just a measurement; it's a sacred pathway, a medium through which the soul experiences growth and transformation. Just as stars are born, burn brightly, and eventually return to the cosmos, our souls move through cycles, each experience bringing us closer to a fuller understanding of ourselves and our connection to the divine.

Living with Eternity in Mind

When we consider the soul as eternal, it changes how we live each day. The choices we make, the love we share, and the challenges we face all become part of a larger journey. We're not simply living for this moment but for something timeless, something that carries on beyond us. This awareness invites us to live with intention, kindness, and purpose, knowing that each action reverberates far beyond our immediate lives.

Living with eternity in mind encourages us to focus on what truly matters, to let go of the trivial, and to cultivate a sense of peace, love, and wisdom that endures. In this way, each day becomes a sacred opportunity to contribute to the journey of our soul, a step along the path of becoming closer to the divine.

Reflections on the Eternal Soul

1. **What does the idea of an eternal soul mean to you?** Reflect on how viewing the soul as timeless might influence the way you see your life, choices, and experiences.

2. **How can you live with eternity in mind?** Think about the ways you can bring more purpose, compassion, and love into each day, knowing that each moment contributes to your soul's journey.

3. **Consider the idea of consciousness as energy.** How does this perspective align with your beliefs about the soul, and what possibilities does it open up for life beyond the physical?

Chapter 21: Science and Spirit in the Dance of Eternity

"The more I study science, the more I believe in God." – Albert Einstein

How do science and spirituality converge in their exploration of time, eternity, and existence? Science and spirituality may seem like opposites, yet they are often partners on the journey of understanding. Where science provides us with theories and tools to explore the physical universe, spirituality brings us into contact with the intangible—the sense of purpose, connection, and wonder that goes beyond the material.

In this chapter, we explore how science and spirituality, when woven together, deepen our appreciation for time, eternity, and the mysteries of existence. **If God is time, as this book suggests, then the universe itself is a physical expression of the divine, operating within time, space, and matter**—a dance of eternity that is both seen and unseen.

The Scientific Perspective: Time, Space, and the Infinite

From a scientific perspective, time is a measurable phenomenon, but it's also full of mystery. **Einstein's theory of relativity** showed us that time isn't static; it's interwoven with space, bending and stretching in response to mass and energy. This suggests that time is not a constant but a flexible, dynamic aspect of reality, influenced by gravity and motion.

Consider the concept of black holes, where the gravitational force is so immense that time slows down dramatically. For someone outside a black hole, time seems to progress normally, but for someone nearing the event horizon, time almost stands still. This phenomenon challenges our usual understanding of time, showing us that **time itself is a force woven into the very structure of the cosmos**. Could this force be a form of the divine, a presence that shapes reality at every level?

Quantum mechanics further complicates our understanding, suggesting that particles can exist in multiple states simultaneously and only "collapse" into a definite state when observed. This points to a reality where **time and matter aren't fixed but are influenced by perception, interaction, and perhaps even consciousness**.

The Spiritual Perspective: Eternity Beyond the Physical

Spirituality offers an equally compelling view of eternity. In many religious and philosophical traditions, the idea of an eternal soul or consciousness that transcends time is central. The Bible speaks of eternity in terms of unity with God, a state that exists beyond earthly concerns. Eternity is not simply a long stretch of time; it's a dimension that surpasses human understanding, a quality of existence in which the divine and the soul exist harmoniously.

Jesus' words in the Gospel of John, "Before Abraham was, I am" (John 8:58), capture the concept of timelessness—suggesting a state of existence where past, present, and future are unified. In this view, eternity is more than endless time; it is a different plane of being, a connection with the divine that transcends the sequential flow we experience.

The Intersection of Science and Spirituality: The Eternal Dance

Science and spirituality offer different, yet complementary perspectives. While science explores the "how" of existence, spirituality explores the "why." Both, however, lead us to a similar conclusion: **there is more to reality than meets the eye**. The deeper we go into either realm, the more we are confronted with mystery.

In a way, science points us back to spirituality. The farther scientists explore the universe, the more questions arise. What lies beyond the observable universe? What caused the Big Bang? Where does consciousness come from? These questions often echo spiritual inquiries, such as the nature of God, the purpose of life, and the origin of the soul.

By embracing both perspectives, we start to see a dance of eternity. Science provides the framework, the structure of time, space, and matter. Spirituality fills it with meaning, connecting us to a larger story, one that extends beyond the limits of our physical understanding.

Finding Unity in the Unknown

The intersection of science and spirituality teaches us humility, reminding us that we are part of something far greater than ourselves. It encourages us to view **existence as a tapestry woven from both the physical and the spiritual**, each thread revealing something new about the divine mystery.

When we look to science, we find awe in the mechanics of the universe—the precision of gravity, the vastness of space, the complexity of life. When we turn to spirituality, we find awe in the unseen, in the sense of connection that binds us to each other and to the divine. Together, these perspectives remind us that existence is layered with purpose and wonder, a dance that is both intricate and infinite.

Reflections for the Dance of Eternity

1. **What insights do science and spirituality offer you about eternity?** Reflect on how each perspective deepens your understanding of time and existence.

2. **How do you experience timelessness in your life?** Consider moments of stillness, presence, or connection that feel eternal, and think about what they reveal to you.

3. **In what ways do science and spirituality complement each other?** Reflect on how these two perspectives enrich your understanding of life's mysteries.

Chapter 22: The Divine Symphony – Embracing Time, Space, and Matter as One

"Time present and time past are both perhaps present in time future, and time future contained in time past." – T.S. Eliot

Imagine the universe as a vast symphony, each moment, particle, and life a note in a divine composition. As we bring together everything explored so far, we see how time, space, and matter function as instruments in this symphony. Together, they create a melody that resonates within us, reminding us that we're not just part of the universe—we're an integral note in its composition.

This final chapter reflects on how seeing **God as time** reshapes our understanding of existence, purpose, and the interconnectedness of all things. The universe is not static; it is alive, a continuous unfolding of time that brings forth new experiences, new understandings, and new life. Recognizing time as the divine force that shapes, guides, and holds all things together brings an awareness that we, too, are active participants in this cosmic dance.

Time as the Divine Thread in the Tapestry of Existence

Throughout our journey, we've seen time as more than a simple measurement; it's the divine thread that weaves through every moment, giving structure to space and movement to matter. Just as a thread binds a tapestry, time binds us to each other and to every part of existence. This view brings a profound sense of connection, showing that the story of life is continuously unfolding, with each moment woven into the next.

The Bible offers glimpses of this connection, reminding us that "For everything there is a season, and a time for every matter under heaven" (Ecclesiastes 3:1). This suggests that every experience, every relationship, every change is part of a larger, divinely guided pattern.

Matter, Space, and Time as Reflections of the Divine Trinity

Seeing time as God, matter as Jesus, and space as the Holy Spirit opens up a new understanding of the Holy Trinity. Just as time flows continuously, shaping and giving meaning to life, so does God as the eternal presence. Matter, like Jesus, is tangible, real, and connected to the physical world, allowing us to experience the divine through touch, sight, and presence. Space, like the Holy Spirit, is the unseen force that fills, holds, and connects all things.

Together, they create a sacred triad that reflects the structure of existence. This view brings a new dimension to the Trinity, showing it not as an abstract theological concept but as a pattern embedded in the very fabric of reality.

Living in Alignment with Divine Time

Seeing time as divine offers a new way to live—with patience, intention, and purpose. If God is time, then every moment becomes an opportunity to engage with the divine. Each experience, whether joyful or challenging, becomes a step on a path that's part of a greater story.

This view encourages us to trust the flow of time, to embrace the unfolding of our lives with faith and gratitude. In moments of struggle, we can remember that time is both our guide and our teacher, helping us grow, learn, and become who we are meant to be. By aligning with divine time, we're not just moving through life; we're participating in a sacred journey that draws us closer to the divine.

The Legacy of Time and the Eternal Now

The concept of an eternal "now," as reflected in both science and spirituality, reminds us that **all of existence is connected**. Every past experience, every present choice, and every future possibility are woven together, creating a continuity that transcends individual lives. By embracing this view, we find peace in knowing that our actions ripple through time, contributing to a larger legacy.

Living with this awareness allows us to act with compassion, love, and purpose, knowing that we're part of something eternal. Time may move forward, but in every moment, we are connected to both the past and the future, creating a legacy that echoes through eternity.

Closing Reflections on the Divine Symphony

1. **How does seeing time as divine influence your life?** Reflect on how this perspective changes the way you view moments, choices, and challenges.

2. **What role do you feel you play in the divine symphony?** Consider how your unique experiences, relationships, and actions contribute to the greater whole.

3. **How can you live more consciously within the flow of divine time?** Reflect on practices or intentions that help you stay present, grounded, and aligned with the unfolding of time.

Conclusion: Presenting the Case for God as Time, Jesus as Matter, and the Holy Spirit as Space

"The truth is incontrovertible. Malice may attack it, ignorance may deride it, but in the end, there it is."
– Winston Churchill

Ladies and gentlemen of the jury, we've reached the final moments of our case. Over these pages, you've heard arguments, witnessed examples, and followed evidence from both science and scripture, each pointing toward a radical yet unifying idea: **God is Time, Jesus is Matter, and the Holy Spirit is Space**. Today, we stand before you not to impose belief but to offer a possibility—a fresh lens through which to view the divine.

As we close, let's revisit the evidence laid before you, summarizing the main arguments and drawing together the threads of this theory.

God as Time: The Eternal Force

From the very beginning, we posited that **God is Time**, the eternal, all-encompassing presence that governs all of existence. Time itself began with God's word in Genesis, setting into motion the creation and growth of the universe. **Scriptures** such as **Psalm 90:2** tell us, "from everlasting to everlasting, you are God," revealing God as an eternal force, unbound by human limits. Time, like God, is a constant, steady presence that shapes life, moves events, and gives meaning to our existence.

Science supports this view. **Einstein's theory of relativity** shows us a flexible time—one that stretches, bends, and transcends the linear path we perceive. If time operates outside of these earthly limits, could it not be a reflection of the divine? Time governs without being governed, much like the God who, as we've explored, exists outside of creation.

Jesus as Matter: The Embodiment of Creation

We then examined **Jesus as Matter**, the physical embodiment of the divine. In John 1:14, "the Word became flesh," showing us that Jesus represents a divine intersection with the physical world. Through **miracles** like turning water into wine, walking on water, and healing the sick, Jesus demonstrated authority over matter, suggesting that He was more than a mere mortal—He was a manifestation of God's power within the tangible world.

In exploring **quantum mechanics**, we find support for this idea: **matter is not as fixed as we once believed**. Subatomic particles exist in multiple states, changing form in ways that align with Jesus' miracles, where He altered states of matter. Through His resurrection, Jesus Himself showed that matter can be transformed, transcending the physical and hinting at a greater reality—a reality where matter is shaped by a divine presence.

The Holy Spirit as Space: The Divine Presence

Finally, we argued that the **Holy Spirit functions as Space**, a presence that connects, surrounds, and holds all things together. In Genesis, the Spirit of God "hovered over the waters," setting creation into motion, and in Acts, the Holy Spirit filled the disciples, empowering them to carry God's message to all corners of the world. The Holy Spirit is the unseen force that fills space, connecting all aspects of creation and bringing the physical and spiritual realms into unity.

Astrophysics supports this view by revealing that space is not empty—it's filled with energy, gravity, and forces that shape galaxies and expand the universe. Like the Holy Spirit, space is a vital, active medium that gives structure to matter and allows time to unfold. In this view, **God, Jesus, and the Holy Spirit** function as a divine Trinity that parallels the structure of the universe itself.

The Scientific Alignment: A Unified Theory

The beauty of this theory lies in how science and spirituality mirror one another. **Relativity shows us a universe where time and space are interwoven,** creating a fabric that matter bends and shapes. This intertwining of time, space, and matter reflects the interconnectedness of the **Holy Trinity**—God the Father as Time, Jesus the Son as Matter, and the Holy Spirit as Space.

In the **expansion of the universe**, we see echoes of the Spirit's movement. In the **mysteries of quantum mechanics**, we glimpse the transforming power of Jesus. In **the unyielding passage of time**, we feel the eternal presence of God. Together, these insights suggest a grand design, a cosmic truth that brings the spiritual and physical worlds into harmony.

The Final Verdict

The evidence has been presented to you from every angle: scripture, scientific theory, and human experience. We've explored how the **Holy Trinity— God as Time, Jesus as Matter, and the Holy Spirit as Space**—mirrors the fundamental structure of the universe. Through these reflections, a powerful question emerges: could it be that the Trinity represents more than a theological concept, but a cosmic truth?

Ultimately, the decision is yours. But as you consider the theory presented, remember this: time will continue to unfold, matter will transform, and space will expand, just as they always have. Perhaps, in the divine interplay of time, space, and matter, we find not just the building blocks of reality, but the fingerprints of God.

The case has been presented, the evidence laid out. I ask only that you keep an open mind as you journey forward, allowing the possibility that **God is not only with us, but around us, within us, and flowing through every moment we live.**

May this theory inspire you to see life and time as sacred, inviting you to explore, to question, and to connect with the divine mystery that surrounds us all. The final verdict is yours.

Afterword

As I bring this book to a close, I want to share a bit about my journey—the winding path that led me to view God, Jesus, and the Holy Spirit through the lens of **Time, Matter, and Space**. Like many, I grew up with a traditional view of God, a powerful figure perched above the world, observing and intervening as needed. It was a comforting image but, over time, began to feel limited, even distant.

The deeper I explored both **spirituality and science**, the more questions arose. I began to wonder if perhaps we've taken religious texts, especially the Bible, a bit too literally. What if these ancient stories are full of **metaphors and parables**, meant to point us toward something far greater than a superhuman figure in the sky? What if, in holding too tightly to certain interpretations, we've overlooked deeper truths and missed the real essence of God?

This line of questioning led me to a revelation: what if **God exists outside creation as the force that governs all things—Time itself**? Time shapes everything. It's constant, all-encompassing, and it moves all things forward, affecting matter and space alike. From this perspective, **Jesus becomes Matter**—the physical embodiment of the divine in our world—and the **Holy Spirit becomes Space**, the unseen presence that surrounds and fills us.

The more I thought about this concept, the more it resonated. This view of the **Holy Trinity** aligns with both **faith** and **science**—fields that have long seemed at odds, yet perhaps share more in common than we realize. Through writing this book, I hope to offer a fresh perspective that bridges these worlds and encourages you to reconsider your own beliefs.

This book is the culmination of my search for a deeper understanding, a journey that has enriched my life in ways I could never have imagined. My hope is that it inspires you to question, to explore, and to discover a God who is far more vast, intimate, and mysterious than any single interpretation could capture. Whether or not you see God as Time, I hope you walk away with a renewed sense of wonder and a willingness to look beyond the familiar.

Thank you for joining me on this journey.

Made in United States
Troutdale, OR
03/25/2025

30073634R00076